PREPARING ART FOR PRINTING

Revised Edition

Bernard Stone and Arthur Eckstein

PREPARING ART FOR PRINTING

Revised Edition

 VAN NOSTRAND REINHOLD COMPANY

New York   Cincinnati   Toronto   London   Melbourne

Copyright © 1983 by Van Nostrand Reinhold Company Inc.
Library of Congress Catalog Card Number 82-24699
ISBN 0-442-27763-6

Printed in the United States of America
Designed by Arthur Eckstein and Bernard Stone
Demonstration Photos by Nat Messik

Published by Van Nostrand Reinhold Company Inc.
135 West 50th Street
New York, New York 10020

Van Nostrand Reinhold
480 Latrobe Street
Melbourne, Victoria 3000, Australia

Van Nostrand Reinhold Company Limited
Molly Millars Lane
Wokingham, Berkshire, England RG11 2PY

16 15 14 13 12 11 10 9 8 7 6 5 4 3 2 1

Library of Congress Cataloging in Publication Data

Stone, Bernard, 1922-
    Preparing art for printing.

    Includes index.
    1. Printing, Practical—Handbooks, manuals, etc.
2. Graphic arts—Handbooks, manuals, etc. I. Eckstein,
Arthur. II. Title.
Z244.3.S86   1983   686.2′24   82-24699
ISBN 0-442-27763-6

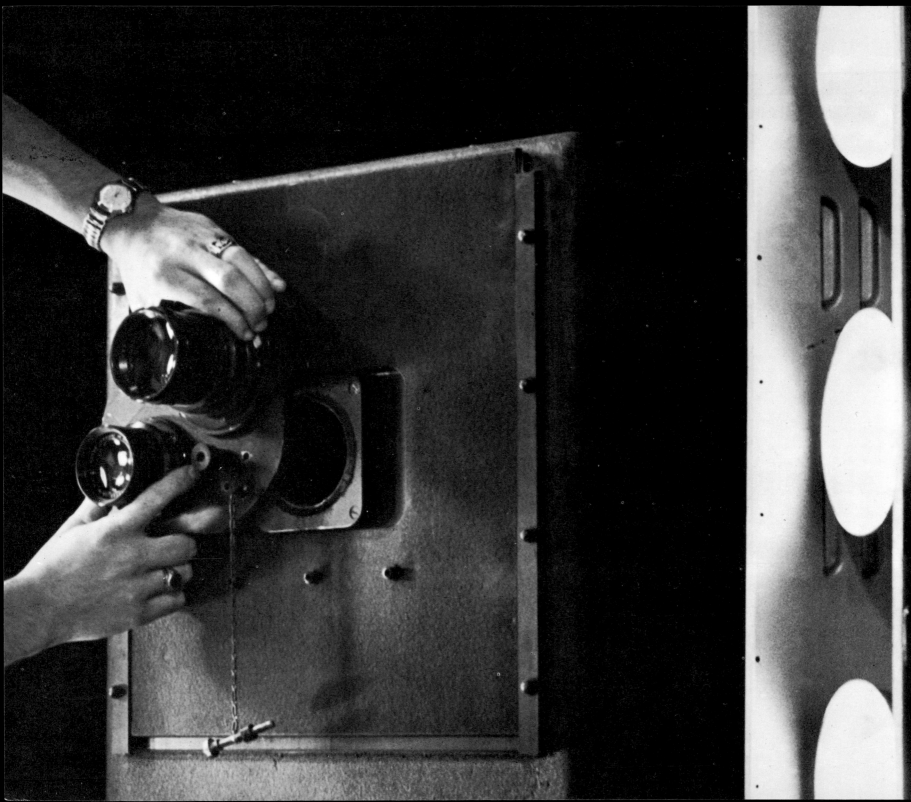

To Annette and Edith

PREFACE   *The graphic artist treads a fine line between the world of creative inspiration and that of technology. In the ability to bridge the two, lies the designer's capacity to realize the fullest potential of his work.   To visualize a project in its final form and to understand simultaneously the transformations through which original art must inevitably pass, is to have consummate understanding of a technology that is evolving at an unprecedented pace. We need not understand all of its nuance, but we must very clearly sense the nature of its process, for then, rather than becoming a hindrance or a barrier to the realization of our efforts, it becomes an effective and flexible tool for the extension of our creative range.   Bernard Stone and Arthur Eckstein draw upon their long professional experience as graphic designers as well as upon their many years as teachers to provide the vehicle through which we may fully understand the nature and complexity of the technology that defines so substantial a portion of graphic design. In their thoughtful and enormously useful book,* **Preparing Art for Printing,** *the authors guide us through the critical relationship between design and technology on a step-by-step odyssey that is a fascinating learning experience. They show us not only how the technology works, but how to communicate with those who manage it, and whose understanding of our needs as designers is so essential to the success of our craft.   This new edition of* **Preparing Art for Printing** *will prove to be an invaluable guide to the student who wishes to understand, for the first time, the nature of the design/production relationship, as it will equally provide the ''old pro'' with new insights into the spectacular evolution of today's amazing graphic technology.*

David C. Levy
Executive Dean
Parsons School of Design

TABLE OF CONTENTS

FOREWORD

It is the function of visual communication to give intelligible graphic form to ideas. The first step is to commit the idea to paper in the form of a rough sketch, an indication of the visual elements to be used to express the idea. The last step is printing, the reproduction of the final visual form which communicates the idea. Between the first step and the last lies the area of professional techniques required to prepare the visual elements, the art, for reproduction. This prepared art is known as the *mechanical;* and it is with the preparation and execution of the mechanical that this book is primarily concerned.

The mechanical represents the artist's ultimate control of the printed result. It determines, to a large extent, the degree of perfection in the printed piece; it tells the platemaker and the printer what to do and, in most cases, directs how it shall be done. The mechanical is a fundamental influence on design thinking.

Mechanicals are prepared by artists, sometimes by the designer of the piece, more often by a specialist in the preparation of art for reproduction. This specialist is variously referred to as a paste-up-artist or mechanical artist. These terms are unfortunate because neither conveys the range of responsibility or expresses the actual importance of this phase of art production. We will refer to the artist responsible for the execution of mechanicals as the *production artist*.

This area of specialization has long been looked down upon as the lowest rung on the ladder of creativity. But the fact is that almost no piece of creative work could ever be reproduced without first being translated into a mechanical. The professional production artist of today is a valuable member of the art staff. His opinion is considered important even during the creative stages of work and his contribution to successful results is of primary significance.

Professional stature must bear the responsibilities of craftsmanship, knowledge and taste. The production artist must be well versed in the procedures and techniques of graphic reproduction and have a high degree of skill with the tools, equipment, and materials of the trade. He must be capable of artistic judgments, decisions involving taste, and understand the visual and verbal language of design and production.

Unlike the formal education available to other professional craftsmen, the production artist's training has traditionally been a period of apprenticeship. The ambitious young artist, whose first job in an art studio was to sweep the floor and fill the paste pots, could learn only by peering over shoulders, asking questions, and practicing on his own. This kind of "training" took time and it predisposed the inexperienced apprentice to adopting the bad habits of others. There were very few school courses developed explicitly to teach the prepara-

tion of art for reproduction and those that were offered proved woefully inadequate.

This situation is being alleviated through the more recent, realistic approaches taken by the art schools and universities. Professional trade organizations, too, are offering more opportunities for specific education. Through these courses, the student can, at least, enter the rapid pace of the graphic arts world as a productive beginner. But it requires experience, further knowledge, and a dedication to craftsmanship to become truly professional.

In presenting this book, it is our purpose to provide the beginner with a foundation of basic knowledge and to equip the professional artist, at any stage of his development, with a comprehensive reference for all the basic processes, tools, and methods involved in the preparation of art for reproduction. The printing processes and the preparation of artwork for reproduction are first dealt with in terms of simple one-color reproduction because a thorough understanding of black-and-white techniques will equip the reader to understand the preparation of art for multi-color printing discussed in the last few chapters. Trade terms are italicized the first time they are used and many are defined.

We will cover each major printing process in sufficient detail to impart the basic knowledge and understanding necessary for the artist. For readers who wish to study these processes in greater technical depth, or to read the fascinating history of printing, there are volumes available on every conceivable aspect of this fabulous industry.

This book will answer most of the "mechanical" questions that arise in the daily operation of an art department. But the production artist will learn early in his career that, in making mechanicals, the exception doesn't prove the rule—the exception is the rule. Therefore, we hope to also provide the understanding necessary to cope with and solve the more unusual problems that always crop up.

The simplified diagram (Figure 1) shows the relative position of the production artist in an average art department. He is the vital link between the creative group and the final product. Everything that is designed for printing must pass through his area of responsibility before it can be reproduced.

The organization of the art department may vary from one firm to another in terms of personnel and titles. A large organization may include, in its "creative" group, an over-all art director, designers, and layout artists, not to mention various specialists, retouchers, illustrators, letterers, etc. Their function is to conceive and express on paper, sketch, the designs and layouts they have created. It is usually their responsibility to specify the typography unless the department has a type director.

The sketch then goes to the production artist who must now prepare the job in the proper, tech-

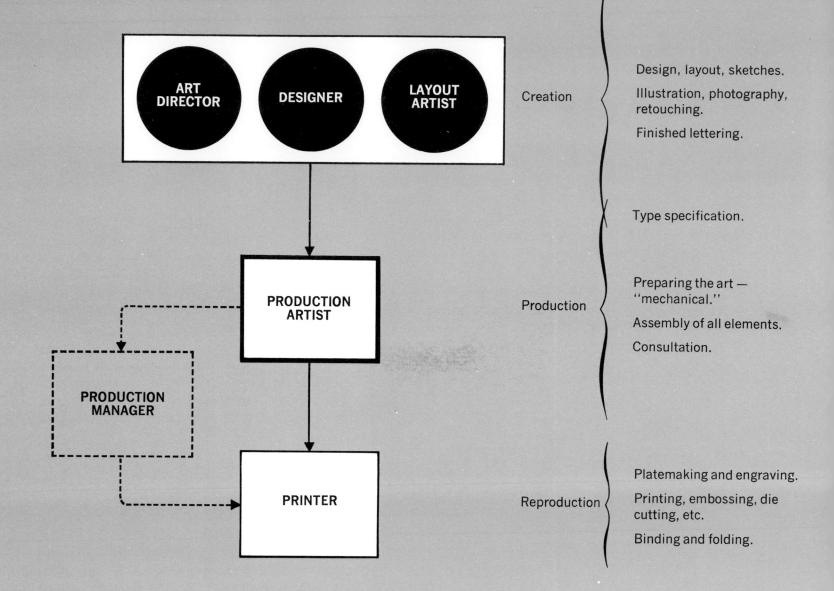

Creation — Design, layout, sketches.
Illustration, photography, retouching.
Finished lettering.

Type specification.

Production — Preparing the art — "mechanical."
Assembly of all elements.
Consultation.

Reproduction — Platemaking and engraving.
Printing, embossing, die cutting, etc.
Binding and folding.

ART DIRECTOR   DESIGNER   LAYOUT ARTIST

PRODUCTION ARTIST

PRODUCTION MANAGER

PRINTER

nically correct form for use by the printer. This prepared form is the mechanical. It is the production artist's responsibility to know which process will be used to reproduce the job, to gather and check all the elements contained in the job, to prepare the mechanical in the most logical and economical form for reproduction, to consult with the designer, art director, or layout artist, and with the printer. When the organization has a production manager on its staff, this last function—liaison with the printers, platemakers, etc.—is within his domain. This requires an intimate familiarity with mechanicals; he must be able to "read" a mechanical to discuss it with the printer. The production manager must have a thorough knowledge of all reproduction processes, the ability to purchase wisely, and handle myriad details, scheduling, and traffic.

It must be understood, however, that very often, especially in the smaller firms, the art director is a one-man department, both art director and designer, and frequently production artist as well.

Organization of a typical art department.

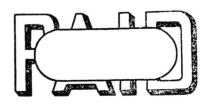 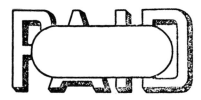 

2 The thumb print and the impression from a rubber stamp are examples of simple direct printing. Many copies of each can be made by inking and pressing to paper.

CHAPTER 1

PRINTING PROCESSES

The preparation of art and copy for reproduction means, quite simply, that work is being prepared for printing. The prepared art is known as a mechanical. The individual responsible for this preparation must understand how the mechanical is translated into a printing plate and how the plate transfers ink to paper. This knowledge is essential for every artist concerned with the graphic arts, whether he is responsible for the initial concept of a piece, its design, or the mechanical from which reproduction starts. The art director and designer must know the reproduction processes in order to take the fullest advantage of printing's versatile capabilities and to avoid going beyond its limitations. The same knowledge permits the production artist, who is the direct link between creation and reproduction, to make correct decisions, decisions that can result in savings at almost every step of the platemaking and printing processes. He should be intimately familiar with the three major printing processes—letterpress, offset lithography, and gravure. He should also have a good understanding of such processes as silk-screening, flexography, thermography, steel die and copperplate engraving, embossing and die-cutting, for he will come into contact with them sooner or later.

A brief definition of printing is the act of transferring ink from one surface to another. Basically there is only one way to do this: by contact under pressure (Figure 2).

When the initial printing surface is a metal plate, which is usually the case in commercial printing, the fundamental printing procedure consists of coating the plate with a layer of ink and then bringing the plate into contact with paper under pressure. The resulting inked impression is the printed image.

Most printing presses in use today, from relatively small offset duplicators to gargantuan rotary newspaper presses, fall into three basic categories of printing: letterpress, offset lithography, and gravure. Despite the distinct differences between these processes, they do have some basic common denominators. Each uses a metal plate. In each case, paper is the most common material used to receive the inked impression.

Although there are areas of overlap, each process has its own specific qualities, its own advantages and limitations, which affect basic considerations of design and art preparation. We will discuss them now in terms of one-color reproduction.

LETTERPRESS—RELIEF PRINTING

Letterpress is a relief process, the oldest form of printing. It comes from the art of woodcutting in which areas not meant to print are gouged out of the wood block, leaving a design that stands in relief. The surface of this raised design is inked, then pressed against paper. The paper now has an ink impression of the original design (Figure 3). These

3 A woodcut and its printed image.

two steps in woodcutting—making a relief printing plate, then pressing the inked plate directly against paper—are still the principles on which relief printing is based. They clearly distinguish letterpress from gravure or lithography.

Letterpress printing, then, is always produced from a relief printing surface, a single printing plate or a combination of one or more plates and type. The plate is usually metal and its relief design is formed by a *photoengraving* process discussed in the next chapter. The metal type achieves its relief characteristic through casting or molding rather than engraving.

The plate, or combination of plates and type, is inked automatically by a roller (Figure 4), then brought into contact with paper under pressure. The result is a letterpress print.

How Letterpress Works

Although the printing procedure is basically simple, many varieties of presses have been developed to accommodate the wide range of letterpress jobs. All these presses, however, operate on the same principle: transferring ink from a relief printing surface directly to the material to be printed. They can be divided into three general classes: platen, flat-bed, and rotary. To see how the basic theory of letterpress printing is applied on these presses, let us follow their printing procedures.

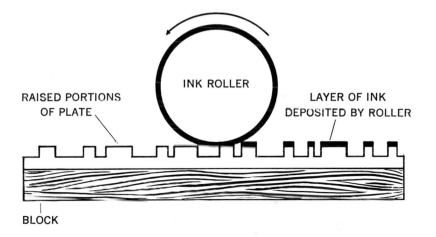

RAISED PORTIONS OF PLATE

INK ROLLER

LAYER OF INK DEPOSITED BY ROLLER

BLOCK

4 Inking the relief printing plate. This cross-section shows clearly why the paste-like ink is deposited only on the raised portions of the plate.

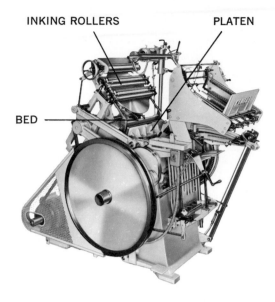

5 Automatic platen press. (KLUGE)

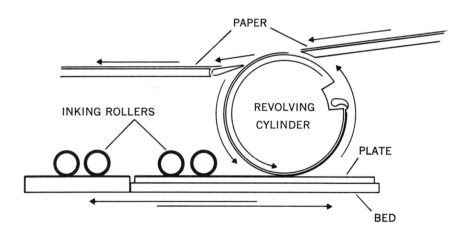

6 Simplified diagram of a flat-bed cylinder letterpress.

PLATEN PRESS. This press (Figure 5) has two flat surfaces, a bed, which supports the printing plate; and a platen which supports the paper. Bed and platen open and close much like a clam. While closed, the platen presses the paper against the inked plate; while open, the print is ejected, the plate is re-inked, and new paper is accepted. The press is usually *sheet-fed* and prints a single color. It can print on *stock* that ranges from thin paper to heavy cardboard and can also be used for embossing, die-cutting and scoring.

FLAT-BED CYLINDER PRESS. Here, the paper is wrapped around a large revolving cylinder, and the plate is locked on a flat bed which moves back and forth. One movement carries the plate under the ink rollers, the other under the cylinder. The paper is printed by the pressure of the revolving cylinder against the inked plate during the forward movement of the bed. The cylinder then rises to permit the bed to slide back under the ink rollers. By the time the plate has been inked and the bed has again moved forward, *grippers* on the cylinder have released the printed sheet and accepted a new sheet (Figure 6).

The press is generally sheet-fed and accepts paper of coarse to fine quality. There are both single-color and two-color models, which are used for printing jobs such as folders, broadsides, pamphlets, catalogs and books.

ROTARY PRESS. Its name comes from the use of two rotating cylinders, a plate cylinder and an impression cylinder. The printing surface, which is a semi-cylindrical relief plate made by molding from the original plates and type, is locked on the plate cylinder. The stock is printed as it passes between the inked plate cylinder and the impression cylinder. Rotary presses are sheet-fed, or *web-fed*—from a roll of paper that is cut into sheets after printing— and range from single-color to six-color models (Figure 7). These extremely accurate, high-speed presses are used for long production runs, i.e., for printing jobs that require a great number of copies such as newspapers, magazines, catalogues and packaging.

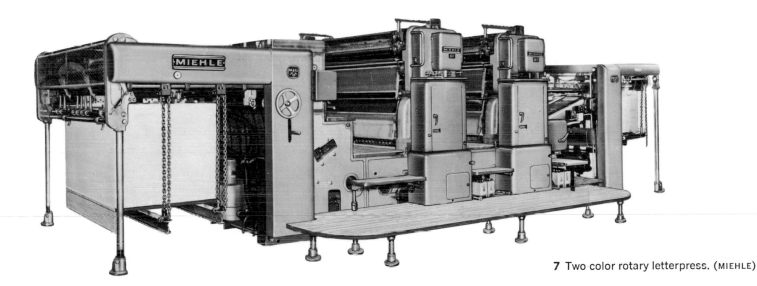

7 Two color rotary letterpress. (MIEHLE)

Generally speaking, quality letterpress printing requires the use of smooth, coated stock. This is due to lack of resiliency, "give," in both the printing and pressure surfaces. The sharpest, most detailed print is produced when these two unyielding surfaces are brought together with a light, even pressure, a "kiss" on paper that has been given a smooth and relatively non-absorbent coating. When rough or textured paper is used, the ideal, light pressure deposits ink only on the raised parts of the unevenly surfaced paper; the result is a "washed out" looking print that lacks detail. If the pressure is increased enough to force ink down into the hollows of the paper, the ink spreads and the result is a print that looks "muddy". Newspapers have adapted the rotary letterpress for printing on coarse, absorbent paper by making the surface of the impression cylinder resilient.

*   *   *

So far, we have discussed the basic principles of letterpress printing as well as the operation of the three types of presses used. However, putting ink on paper is only one of the many steps necessary to translate a mechanical into a printed piece.

1. Typesetting. Manuscript copy is set in type. In letterpress this almost always means metal type, which is set, or composed, by a compositor in a composing room. He can set type entirely by hand, partly by hand and partly by machine, or entirely by machine. Type is discussed in more detail in Chapter 3, at this point we need only know that all metal type is cast to a standard height, 0.918 inch.

2. Photoengraving. Artwork is photoengraved on a thin sheet of metal (see Chapter 2). When used alone, a photoengraving is a printing plate that can be used just as it is. But when one or more photoengravings are to be printed with metal type, the surface height of the photoengravings must be raised to match the standard surface height of the type. This is done by *blocking,* attaching the photoengraved plate to a wood or metal base.

3. Makeup. Engravings and type are assembled in a metal frame called a *chase,* in the positions indicated by the layout or mechanical, then locked in position to prevent movement of individual pieces; when a locked unit is placed on the press for printing, it is called a *form.* A form holds all engravings and type that are to be printed on one side of one sheet, and may be anything from a one-page ad to 32 pages of a pamphlet or book. The positioning of pages in a form is governed by an imposition, which is a layout of pages so arranged that they will be in proper sequence when the printed sheet is folded and trimmed.

4. Make-ready. The final adjustment of plates and type on the printing press to ensure a perfect impression is the make-ready. It is a precise and often time-consuming job but it is essential to fine presswork.

5. Press-ready. This is the adjustment of the press itself to the requirements of the job—changing ink, adjusting paper guides and any attachments that are to be used for the job. After press-ready is completed, printing starts.

After printing is done, the inked-sheets are dried and trimmed to their proper size, or folded and bound, or put through any other operation the job may require.

6. Proofing. Proofs are trial prints made on a small hand press. When proofs are pulled from metal type still in a *galley* they are called galley proofs, from photoengravings—engraver's proofs; and from assembled type and cuts—page proofs. These proofs serve as check points for platemaker, typesetter, printer and customer. A press-proof is a print made on the actual printing press, used as a preview of how the printed job will look. A repro-duction proof is a proof of the finest quality, pulled on a hand press for use as original artwork.

7. Duplicate Plates. These are just what the name implies. They can be made of metal, plastic or rub-ber, from type, photoengravings or a combination of both. They are used to save wear-and-tear on type and original engravings during a long press run; to permit the identical plates to be used in a number of places at the same time. A *stereotype* is the cheapest duplicate plate. It is made from a paper or plastic mold (mat) and primarily used for news-paper printing. An *electrotype* is the best duplicate plate and is the one most commonly used.

PHOTO-OFFSET LITHOGRAPHY
PLANOGRAPHIC PRINTING

Planographic refers to any process that prints from a plane surface, one that is neither raised in relief, nor incised; the image simply rests on the surface of the plate as an ink attracting area (Figure 8).

Lithography, which is based on the principle that grease and water do not mix, is the best-known form of planographic printing and the newest of the three major processes. It stems from the art of drawing with a greasy crayon on the flat surface of a certain type of limestone. When the surface of the stone is flushed with water and then inked, the greasy crayon areas reject the water but retain the oily ink, while the blank stone areas retain the water but reject the ink. The print, made by pressing paper directly against the inked surface is a mirror-image reproduction of the design on the stone.

Although hand drawing on stone has changed to photoprinting on sensitized metal, and direct printing is now used almost exclusively as an art medium, modern lithography is still identified by its characteristic plane surface and the principle that grease and water do not mix.

Today's commercial process is photo-*offset* lithography, an indirect printing method. It shares the identifying characteristics of direct lithography but it is further set apart by its own offset characteristic: transferring ink from the plate to an intermediate rubber-blanketed cylinder, which in turn transfers, offsets, the ink to the paper.

How Offset Works

All offset printing is done on rotary presses based on the three-cylinder principle (Figures 9, 10, 11). The presses are made in many sizes and models, from small one-color, sheet-fed offset duplicators to huge, five-color, 72-inch-wide, web-fed presses.

The printing surface is a single planographic plate chemically sensitized to accept ink and reject water in the printing areas, and to accept water and reject ink in the non-printing areas. But to better understand offset printing, let us follow the basic procedures on a single-color press.

The thin metal plate carries an image that is a replica of the original design except, perhaps, in

8 Cross-section of an inked lithography plate.

9 One-color offset press. (MIEHLE)

10 Four-color sheet-fed offset press. (CONSOLIDATED CHAMPION)

11 Multiple-color web-fed offset press. (MIEHLE)

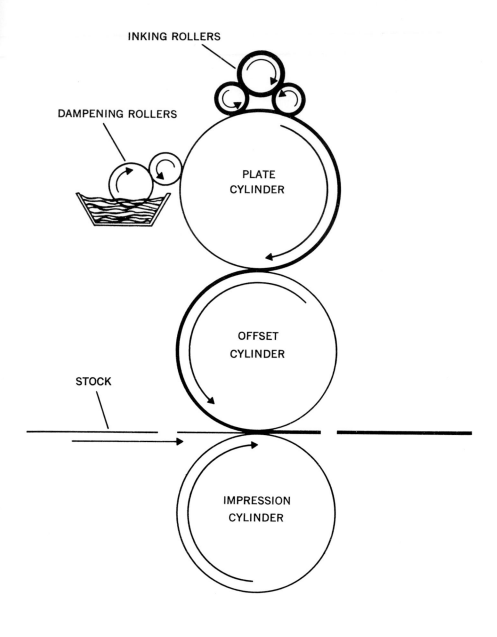

INKING ROLLERS

DAMPENING ROLLERS

PLATE
CYLINDER

OFFSET
CYLINDER

STOCK

IMPRESSION
CYLINDER

12 Simplified diagram of an offset lithography press.

size. It is wrapped around the plate cylinder and prepared for printing by two sets of rollers. One set wets the plate, the other set inks it. The water is retained only in the non-printing areas, while the ink is retained only in the printing areas. As the plate cylinder rotates against the rubber-blanketed offset cylinder, the inked image on the plate is printed on the blanket. The image on the blanket is now a mirror image of the original design. The offset cylinder rotates against the impression cylinder, which carries the paper, and offsets the image onto the paper (Figure 12). The image on the paper, the final print, is, again, a replica of the original design.

The major steps that took place before and after printing are listed below:

1. Typesetting. Manuscript copy is set in type usually by some phototypesetting method, or in metal (see Chapter 3). Offset lithography, unlike letterpress, cannot use metal type as such, since the printing plate is flat. Reproducing by offset type requires some form of printed matter such as photoprints from phototypesetting or paper proofs printed from metal type. In cither case, the final type used for reproduction is referred to as a *reproduction proof* or *repro.*

2. Photography. Both illustrations and type matter are photographed on film to the exact size planned for the final print.

3. Make-up. The films are stripped (assembled) into their layout positions on a specially coated yellow or orange masking sheet called *goldenrod*.

4. Make-ready. This final checkup to ensure the best possible impression is a simpler procedure in offset than in letterpress since the single offset plate requires fewer adjustments.

5. Press-ready. Adjusting the press to the requirements of the job involves the same essential steps as those for letterpress. Steps after printing are also essentially the same.

6. Proofing. Proofs here serve the same purpose as in letterpress. However, offset proofs are photoprints made from film (the flat) usually blueprints, and only show the position of the elements and not the plate or printing quality. A press proof pulled from the plate itself is rather expensive since the actual press (not a hand proofing press) must be used.

7. Duplicate Plates. No duplicate plates are made. When another plate is needed, a new one is made directly from the flat.

Offset lithography has an advantage in its ability to achieve fine printing on rough or textured stock —the resilient rubber blanket compensates for variations in paper thickness and texture. Reproduction, although sharp and clear to the naked eye, is softer than letterpress since printing is from a plane image on the rubber blanket and is done with far less pressure.

GRAVURE—INTAGLIO PRINTING

The gravure printing surface (Figure 13) is the opposite of the letterpress surface. The printing image is incised rather than raised in relief. Gravure is an adaptation of the hand art of metal engraving or etching—intaglio—in which the artist uses a sharp tool or acid to incise the lines he wants to print. Ink is forced into these lines and the non-printing surface wiped clean so that ink remains only in the depressed image areas. A print is made by placing paper on the plate under enough pressure to lift the ink out of the incised lines.

Commercial gravure is known as rotogravure because all printing is done on rotary presses. The intaglio printing plate is a permanent metal cylinder that is mounted on the press for printing. It prints by transferring ink from wells of varying depth directly to the paper.

13 Cross-section of a gravure (intaglio) printing surface.

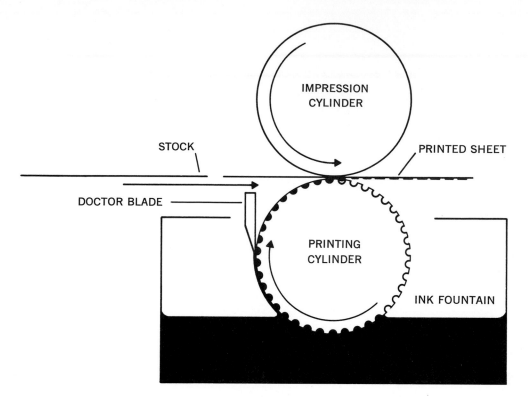

STOCK

IMPRESSION
CYLINDER

PRINTED SHEET

DOCTOR BLADE

PRINTING
CYLINDER

INK FOUNTAIN

14 Simplified diagram of gravure printing.

How Rotogravure Works

The printing procedure on a rotogravure press involves two cylinders: an etched printing cylinder—the printing plate; and an impression cylinder. The printing cylinder revolves in a fountain of ink while a *doctor blade,* in constant contact with the cylinder, wipes all ink from its surface. The ink is left only in the etched image areas, the wells in the plate (Figure 14). The paper is printed by suction, which draws the ink out of the wells to the paper, as it passes between the plate cylinder and the impression cylinder (Figure 15).

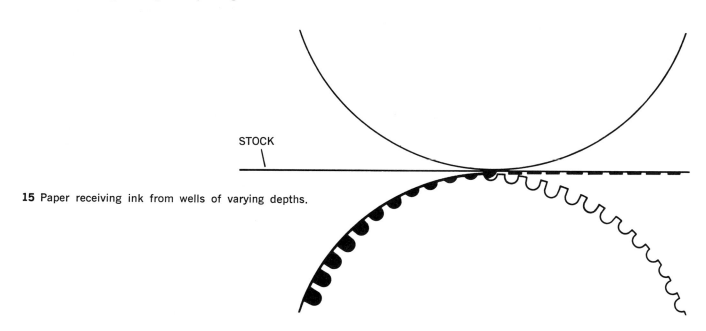

STOCK

15 Paper receiving ink from wells of varying depths.

The major steps that take place before and after printing are highlighted below:

1. Typesetting. Composition and typesetting is accomplished in the same manner as in offset lithography.

2. Photography. Artwork and type are photographed on film.

3. Makeup. The film is assembled on a glass-topped table as indicated by mechanicals and page imposition. The printing image is transferred to the cylindrical plate photomechanically through use of an intermediate carbon tissue. (Steps 2 and 3 are part of the gravure platemaking process described in Chapter 2.)

4. Press-ready, proofing, trimming, etc., are essentially the same as in offset.

Gravure is capable of producing deep, rich tonal values because the tones are printed in ink densities. It has the advantage of quality reproduction even on absorbent newsprint, and also prints effectively on both textured and smooth surfaces.

The rotary presses are almost all web-fed and very large, with some multi-color presses ranging up to 150 inches wide (Figure 16). Because of its outstanding speed, gravure is practical for long runs. It is used for publication printing, catalogs, packaging, printing on cellophane and foil, and even the printing of floor coverings. Sheet-fed presses are used mainly for reproducing works of art and for some advertising literature.

16 Sheet-fed gravure press. (CHAMPLAIN)

SILK-SCREEN PRINTING

Silk-screen printing is one of the most adaptable and versatile reproduction processes in use today. It is used for fine art reproduction, posters and displays and for decorative printing on fabric and wallpaper. It is capable of printing on paper, cardboard, wood, glass, plastics and metal; in addition, the printing form can be fitted to print on bottles, jars, cans or molded pieces of unusual shape. Silk-screen printing is done with either ink or paint.

The printing "plate" in the silk-screen process is a fine-mesh material tightly stretched over a wood or metal frame. The screen material can be of silk, nylon, or metal such as stainless steel, copper, etc. The printing image is achieved by closing the meshes of the screen in the areas that are not to print and, conversely, leaving open those portions that are to print. The blocking out of the non-printing areas is done with a stencil, which can be either cut by hand or prepared photographically. In either case the stencil is adhered to the screen to form the printing image. To make an impression the frame is placed, screen side down, on the surface to be printed. Ink or paint is poured into the frame then drawn across the screen with a rubber squeegee to force the color through the open meshes. When the screen is raised, the printed image is on the stock (Figure 17).

One of the distinguishing features of the process is that the deposit of ink is much heavier and thicker than is possible with any other printing method. Thus the silk-screen process affords great brilliance and opacity of color, makes possible the printing of light colors on dark backgrounds, and is an excellent medium for printing fluorescent and metallic colors, lacquers, and even glue.

Although a great deal of silk-screen work is still done by hand, many automatic presses of varying

17 Composite illustration of the silk-screen process.

sizes and designs have been developed to accommodate the special applications and the wide range of normal work produced by this process.

FLEXOGRAPHY

Flexographic printing is basically a form of letterpress printing. It differs in two respects: it uses a liquid ink rather than the paste type used in letterpress; and although the printing is done from a relief image, the plates are made exclusively of rubber. This process is used mainly for roll-to-roll printing. The stock is fed into the press from a roll and emerges as a printed continuous roll. It can print on practically any web-fed material that can pass through a press. The process is also practical for both short and long runs.

Because of the fluidity of the ink, flexography is ideally suited to hard-surfaced materials such as cellophane, foil, polyethylene and other plastic films, and glossy papers. Flexography cannot be used on highly absorbent papers because such stock consumes too much of the very fluid ink and thus makes the job uneconomical. The process is not used for fine-detail reproduction because the ink has a tendency to overflow, but it is well suited to printing large solid areas and bright colors. Because flexographic inks are highly pigmented and fully opaque, the process is in general use for such things as candy bar wrappers, grocery and retail bags, milk cartons, food packaging, and gift wraps.

THERMOGRAPHY

This process is not actually printing; it is a method of producing a raised image on an already printed sheet. The thermography machine can be used in conjunction with any standard printing press since no special dies or plates are required. Thermography consists of dusting the printed image, while the ink is still wet, with a powdered compound that has a low melting point. The surplus powder that does not adhere to the wet ink is removed by a vacuum. The printed image, which is now covered with powder, passes through a heating unit and then is cooled. The final effect is a raised, printed image. This can be achieved in most colors, either dull or gloss, and in white, gold, silver or copper.

STEEL DIE AND COPPERPLATE ENGRAVING

This process is identified by two features. The printed image is usually raised; and the process is capable of reproducing extremely fine detail. Steel die engraving is a form of intaglio printing since the printing image is sunken, engraved, below the surface of the plate. The engraved plate is a female die which contains the ink. A male die is made and when the two are pressed together with the paper in between, the result is an embossed, inked reproduction of the engraved plate. For long runs, a steel die is made; for short runs, less expensive copper is used. The process is especially suitable for letterheads, announcements, and cards.

EMBOSSING

Embossing produces a raised or relief image. When embossing is done on blank stock, it is called *blind embossing*. It can also be done in register with a printed image. Embossing is achieved by using a female brass die and a male counter, both of which are mounted in register on a press. The counter is actually an impression made from the die and is the only raised area on the bed of the press so that pressure will be applied only in the die area. The embossed image is produced by pressing the stock between the die and the counter. Light embossing may be done without heat. For heavy embossing and fine detail, the press is equipped with a heated plate to which the die is fastened.

DIE CUTTING

Die cutting is cutting stock to a predetermined shape, either regular or irregular, on the perimeter of the piece or inside the work itself. Cutting dies are usually simple constructions. The outline to be die-cut is traced and jigsawed into a block of plywood; a strip of steel with a sharp cutting edge is bent to fit and inserted into the jigsawed track, projecting one-quarter inch above the wood base. The die form is then locked onto the bed of a printing or die-cutting press and the stock is cut as it is fed through the press. Die-cutting can be done on a platen press or a flat-bed cylinder press.

CHAPTER 2

THE PLATEMAKING PROCESS

Craftsmen

18 Examples of line copy.

The printing processes we have just discussed are, for the most part, the last steps in the reproduction sequence. But before printing can occur, a printing plate must be made. A separate chapter is devoted to platemaking because it is probably the most important step for the artist to understand thoroughly. For it is the printing plate that largely determines the quality of the reproduction; and it is here, through the mechanical, that the artist can exert a direct influence on the printed result, both in quality and in cost. We start with some form of *copy* for single-color reproduction.

COPY

Copy refers to any material that is to be reproduced (printed). It is the artwork from which a printing plate will be made and includes type proofs, drawings, photographs, mechanicals, etc. Copy is divided into two basic categories: *line and continuous tone*.

Line Copy

Material that has no gradations in tone; the design being formed by solid-black lines, dots, or areas: pen or brush-and-ink drawings, type proofs, typewritten material; areas of solid color; crosshatching or stippling; ruled lines; scratchboard; etc. (Figure 18).

Continuous-tone Copy

Material in which gradations of tone occur in an uninterrupted flow: photographs; pencil or pastel drawings, paintings in all media; airbrush work, etc. (Figure 19).

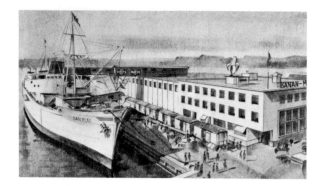

19 Examples of reproduction from continuous-tone copy.

PRINTING PLATES

Each of the major reproduction processes commonly uses a metal plate as its printing surface. *Platemaking* is the generic term applied to the process of producing a metal printing surface from prepared artwork. More specifically, the term refers to lithographic or gravure plates. For letterpress plates, the process is known as photoengraving.

Photoengraving for Letterpress— The Relief Printing Plate

The most common metals used for letterpress engravings are copper, for fine work and long runs; zinc, for short runs and less exacting reproduction; and magnesium, for its combined advantages of light weight, good press life, and reproduction quality. In recent years, many advances have been made in the manufacture of printing plates, including light-weight plastic printing plates, and chrome-plated plates that can make runs of over two million impressions.

There are three basic kinds of letterpress plates: line, *halftone* and *combination*.

THE LINE ENGRAVING — REPRODUCING LINE COPY. The first step in making a line plate is photographic. Original line copy is fastened to a copyboard in front of the engraver's camera and illuminated (Figure 20). The camera is focused to enlarge or reduce the film image to the exact size of the final reproduction. The film used by the en-

20 Engraver's camera and copy board.

graver is insensitive to values of gray; it can register only solid black and white. Line copy will produce a film negative with completely opaque background areas, which will become the non-printing areas of the plate, and fully transparent image areas. The transparent areas will become the printing surface of the plate.

The film negative is stripped from its supporting base and turned over to reverse the image left for right. This reversal is necessary since the image will again be reversed in position during the printing process. The negative is then placed on a sheet of plate glass, called a *flat*. (For economy of production, several line negatives may be joined or assembled on the same flat to go through the steps of the engraving process simultaneously.) The flat is placed face down on a metal plate which has been given a light-sensitive coating. Flat and plate are placed in a vacuum frame from which the air is exhausted to ensure perfect contact between film and metal. An exposure made with a powerful arc lamp projects light through the transparent portions of the negative to affect corresponding portions of the light-sensitive coating on the metal plate. The plate is then developed and "fixed" to make the areas that have been exposed to light, the printing image, acid resistant. The rest of the coating is washed away during development, leaving the non-printing areas unprotected metal.

The metal plate is now given several acid baths or bites which etch away the unprotected background areas and leave the acid resistant printing surfaces in relief. Between bites, the sides and edges of the raised portions must be protected to prevent undercutting by the acid. A fine resinous powder, Dragon's Blood, is brushed onto the plate and the plate is heated to melt and fuse the powder which then becomes acid resistant. This is done four times, each time brushing in a different direction to fully protect all exposed edges.

After the acid etching has been completed, the nonprinting portions of the plate are mechanically routed, gouged out, to even greater depths and the plate is mounted on a wood base or block. The combined height of the metal plate and the wood block is .918″, exactly type high. The finished engraving is printed on a proof press to check it against the original (Figure 21).

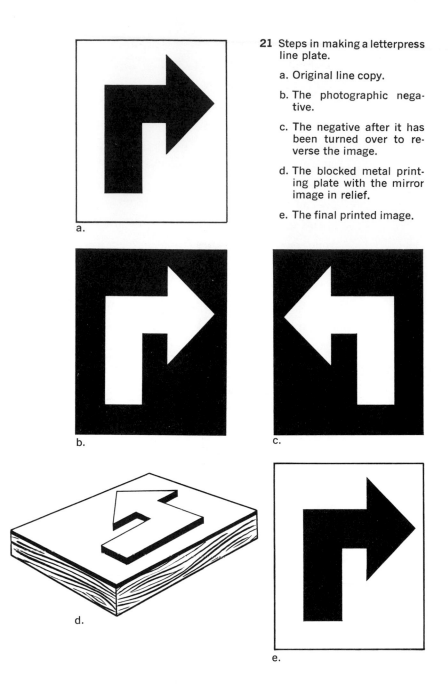

21 Steps in making a letterpress line plate.

a. Original line copy.

b. The photographic negative.

c. The negative after it has been turned over to reverse the image.

d. The blocked metal printing plate with the mirror image in relief.

e. The final printed image.

THE HALFTONE ENGRAVING—REPRODUCING CON-TINUOUS-TONE COPY. Continuous-tone copy is reproduced by the halftone process. All gradations of tone, from very light gray to solid black, are achieved with one plate, one constant ink color, and one pass through the press. In order to reproduce the tonal gradations in continuous-tone copy, the image is broken into a series of dots of varying size, all of which print solid black. The difference in the size of these tiny dots and the amount of white paper that shows between them produces visual mixtures of black and white that are perceived as gradations in tone that correspond to those in the original copy. Where the gray tone is light in the original copy, the black dots in the reproduction will be quite small, thus allowing more

of the white paper to show. As the gray tone becomes darker, the dots grow larger, begin to touch and merge, allowing less and less of the paper to show. When the dots have fully merged, no white paper can be seen, and the result is solid black (Figure 22).

These dot structures are formed by means of the halftone screen. Its use is the basic difference between line and half-tone reproductions. The screen is composed of two sheets of glass, each having etched lines that are equally spaced, parallel, and opaque. Both sheets are cemented together with the ruled sides facing each other and the lines crossing at right angles. The fineness of the screen is determined by the number of lines per inch. A coarse screen of 50 lines to the inch will reproduce

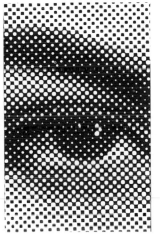

22 a. Reproduction of continuous-tone copy without using the halftone screen.

b. The halftone screen.

c. Halftone reproduction of the same continuous-tone copy.

d. An enlargement of the halftone dot formation showing the variation of dot sizes.

23 Cameraman holding a half- tone screen.

a. Reproduced with a 50- line halftone screen.

b. 85-line screen.

c. 120-line screen.

fewer dots in a given area, therefore a coarser image, than a fine screen of 120 lines to the inch. The screen selected is determined by the detail of the subject, the type of stock on which it is to be printed, and the printing equipment used. For example, a coarse screen, 50-65 lines, is used in halftone reproduction for newspapers because news print is soft, rough and absorbent. Better grades of hard-surfaced glossy papers can accommodate finer screens. Halftone screens for extremely fine reproduction run as high as 300 lines to the inch (Figure 23).

Before the cameraman photographs the continuous-tone copy, he places the halftone screen in the camera, in front of the film. He has already focused the image to the size of the final reproduction. During the exposure the light reflected from the copy must pass not only through the lens but also through the mesh of tiny windows created by the halftone screen before it reaches the film. As a result, the film, which is sensitive only to black and white, records the amount of light passing through each window in the form of a solid dot. The size of each dot is determined by the amount of light reflected from a corresponding point on the original art (Figure 24).

The negative is developed, cut to size, stripped from its backing, and placed on the glass flat just as in line work. Assemblies of various negatives

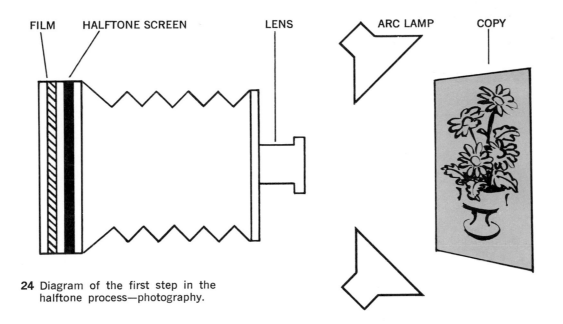

FILM   HALFTONE SCREEN   LENS   ARC LAMP   COPY

24 Diagram of the first step in the halftone process—photography.

can be made at this point. The flat and the light-sensitized plate are placed in the photoprinting machine, a vacuum is created for perfect contact, and the exposure made. The plate is developed and etched with a series of bites very similar to those in line engraving. However, acid etching on halftone plates must be more carefully done, because the plate must retain a series of many small dots without undercutting or changing their size. Any change in the size of the dots alters the tonal values in the reproduction. After the first bite, portions of the plate that have been sufficiently etched are covered with an acid resistant ink so that the rest of the plate can go through further acid baths without affecting the finished areas. This is the *staging* process which gives the engraver control over the amount of etching on every portion of the plate. Imperfections are corrected or removed with hand engraving tools and the plate is blocked type high. The halftone engraving is then proofed on a proof press, and proof and plate are checked against the original art for faithful reproduction. Adjustments and corrections can still be made by further etching and engraving.

Halftones can be finished in a number of ways:

1. Square Halftone. This is the simplest and the most common form of halftone. It is square or rectangular and its entire printing surface is completely covered with a halftone dot formation. There are no pure white or solid black areas. Even the white areas of the original will carry a pinpoint dot in the square halftone (Figure 25).

2. Outline or Silhouette Halftone. Any irregular shape can be outlined. The outline can be an arbitrary form or the silhouetting of a specific image. In either case, the full tonal range of the original will exist over the entire halftone image, but all the dots outside the outlined area will be completely removed (Figure 26).

25 Square halftone.

26 Silhouette halftone.

3. Highlight Halftone. Highlights or other pure white areas in the original copy can be duplicated in reproduction by entirely removing the dots in corresponding areas of the film or plate. These dots are either eliminated photographically by the cameraman or tooled out by hand after the plate is made (Figure 27).

4. Vignette Halftone. The halftone dots on the perimeter of a vignette halftone become smaller and smaller until they disappear. This results in a soft, blended edge (Figure 28).

27 Highlight halftone.

28 Vignette halftone.

FLAT TONE—TINTS. A *tint,* in reproduction, gives the impression of a single value, a flat tone of the color being printed. In one-color (black) printing, this would be gray.

The tint is created by a regular pattern of dots. But, unlike the halftone, the dots in a tint are all of equal size (Figure 29). The proportion of black,

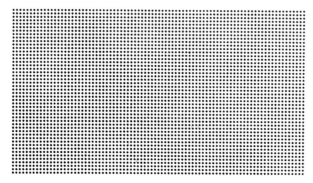

29 Enlarged section of tinted area.

the printed dots, and white, the paper, is constant throughout the tinted area. Each value of gray has its own dot size, which is the same over the entire tint. The smaller the dot, the lighter the gray; the larger the dot, the deeper the gray. These flat tones are specified as percentages of solid black; i.e., 10% black is very light gray; 50% black is a gray exactly halfway between white and black; etc. (Figure 30). Only line copy can be reproduced photomechanically as a flat tone to any specified percentage of black (Figure 31).

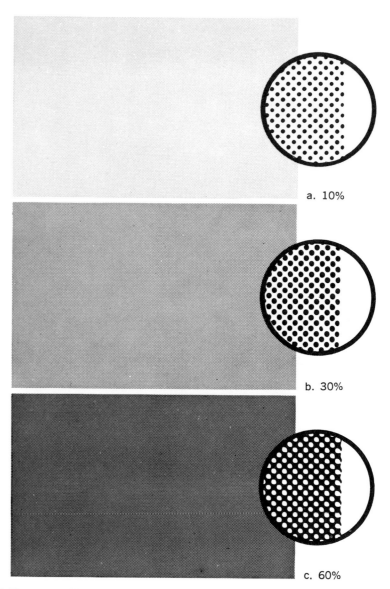

a. 10%

b. 30%

c. 60%

30 Tint areas. Notice that the dot size gets larger as the tint gets darker.

31 a. Reproduction of line copy.

b. Reproduction of the same line copy tinted to 40%.

Benday Process. This was the original process which made it possible for the engraver to convert an area on a relief line plate into a tint. After the line plate was made, the engraver transferred a dot pattern of the proper tint (the Benday screen) against those portions of the plate that were to be tinted. This transferred ink was acid resistant and protected the dot pattern from the acid etching that followed, After etching, the resulting pattern of raised dots reproduced as the desired gray (tint of black).

This original Benday process is virtually obsolete and has been replaced by an in-the-camera screening method on pre-printed film that is more efficient, less costly, easily manipulated by the cameraman and platemaker, and can be applied to *any* platemaking process. The name Benday has been retained through common usage and is occasionally applied to the new methods as well. Today tinting is accomplished with pre screened negative film of the desired tint value. This negative is assembled on the flat directly over the line negative to be tinted, prior to exposure onto the printing plate.

In addition to the normal dot structure for tinting, patterns are available in many line and dot designs (Figure 32). Coarse or fine patterns must be selected on the same basis and with the same consideration as halftone screens. To screen line copy, the same dot patterns can be applied directly to the line negative. An opaque pattern of dots or lines through which light cannot pass during exposure of the plate is placed over the transparent image portion of the negative. The dot pattern laid on a negative is reversed in value so that the print on the metal will be correct.

Shading sheets are also used today. These are transparent plastic sheets on which the dot patterns have been preprinted. The engraver merely cuts a piece to the proper size and assembles it with his negatives on the flat.

COMBINATION ENGRAVINGS. These elements—line, halftone and tints, singly and in combination—comprise every conceivable printing effect.

Black lines and white lines can cross screened areas. Images can be completely reversed in color, from black on white to white on black. Solid areas can be contiguous to screened areas. Halftones may have sections that are pure black, or pure white.

These are a few of the simpler effects that can be achieved; and all are combinations of line with halftones or tints, or all three together.

A photoengraving that combines line and halftone material into one composition on the same printing plate is called a *combination plate*. Line negative and halftone negative are taped together on a flat, in the position indicated by the mechanical or layout. The metal plate is then exposed through this combination. If the line and halftone material overlap in such a way that the negatives cannot be combined on one flat, they are placed on separate flats and exposed in sequence on the same plate. All combination plates require at least two pieces of film. Combination plates are most often used to produce two effects:

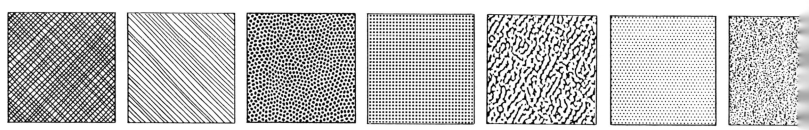

32 Some of the variety of tints and patterns available.

1. Dropout. A dropout is a platemaking procedure which makes it possible to create the visual effect of white line copy over or within a screened background. It is actually the removal or elimination of specified sections of dots within the halftone or flat-tone area (Figure 33).

When a dropout is specified, the halftone copy and the line copy to be dropped out are each photographed as usual to produce film negatives. But the line negative is then converted into a film positive to achieve a clear background and opaque image. When this film positive is placed directly over the halftone negative, the opaque areas of the positive—the original line copy to be dropped out—will not permit light to pass through; consequently, no halftone dots will be formed in this portion of the halftone plate. The result is a pure white dropout. The rest of the halftone negative was unaffected by the transparent background of the film positive and therefore retained its complete dot formation.

a.   b.

c.   d.

33 Dropouts.
a. In tinted area. b. Enlarged section. c. In halftone. d. Enlarged section.

a.   b.

c.   d.

34 Surprints.
   a. In tinted area. b. Enlarged section. c. In halftone. d. Enlarged section.

2. Surprint. A surprint is the exposure of one negative over the exposure of another on the same printing plate. It can achieve the visual effect (among others) of solid black (line copy) within or over a halftone or tint (Figure 34).

The production of a surprint requires a special combination technique. Here the halftone negative and the line negative are always placed on separate flats. After the plate has been exposed through the halftone negative, a second exposure is made on the same plate through the line negative which, of course, has an opaque background and transparent image. Since light can pass only through the transparent sections of the line negative, the result is solid black lines within the halftone area. The opaque background of the line negative covered the rest of the halftone negative and prevented any further exposure of the plate.

When line copy is intended to touch a screened area ("butt" or "kiss" or "flush") the combination plate is handled as a normal surprint (Figures 35 and 36).

35 Other surprint effects.

36 Surprint and dropout on same printing plate.

Blocking. In letterpress printing, the surfaces of all the assembled elements (line plates, halftone and combination plates, type) must all be exactly the same height in order to come into even contact with the paper. Therefore, photoengravings must be fastened to wood or metal *blocks* to equal the height of type slugs.

Mortising. It is sometimes necessary to cut out sections of a plate for corrections, changes, or special fitting needs. An *outside mortise* (or *notch*) is a cut to an edge of the plate leaving an open end. An *inside mortise* is a cut out of any part of the middle of the plate (Figure 37).

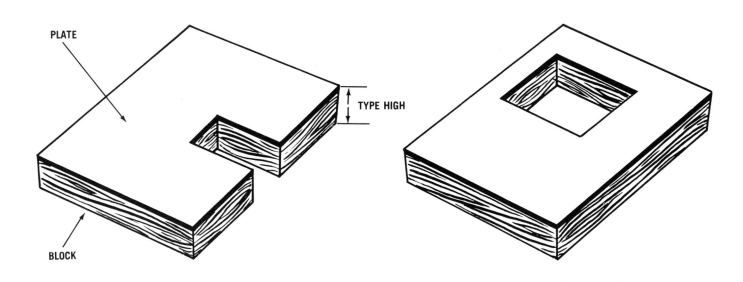

37 a. Outside mortise or notch.

b. Inside mortise.

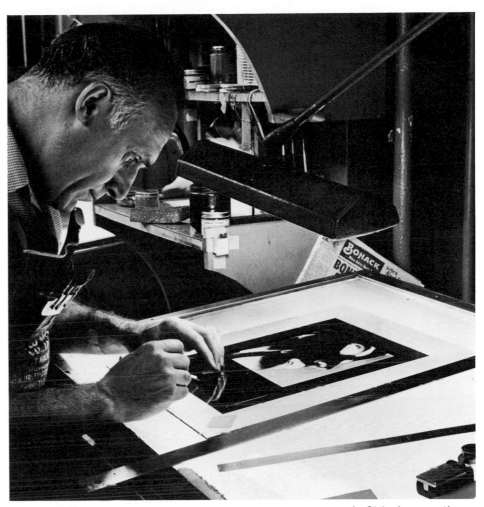

b. Stripping negatives.

38 Photographs taken at engraving plant. (STERLING REGAL)

a. Setting the camera.

c. Exposing the plate.

d. Preparing for etching.

e. Hand finishing.

f. Routing.

g. Proofing.

53

Platemaking For Offset Lithography—
The Planographic Plate

In letterpress printing, presses can accommodate any size plate up to the maximum dimensions of the press bed. In lithography, however, each press can use only one plate size because the plate must be secured to a plate cylinder of constant diameter and length.

Lithography plates are made of zinc, aluminum, or stainless steel and are thin and flexible enough to be curved around the plate cylinder of the press. All copy—line, continuous tone, combinations, etc.—is reproduced with the same plate. There is no printing directly from type.

Artwork for lithographic reproduction is photographed in the same manner as in photoengraving: line copy directly on line film and continuous tone through a halftone screen. Stock developed specifically for offset lithography makes it possible to use fine screens for halftone reproduction. These range from 133 to 300 lines per inch. Each lithographer generally uses only one screen for all his halftone work; the most widely used is 133 lines. Though the etched-glass halftone screen is still used by lithographers, many of them are now using an inexpensive plastic screen which is discarded when damaged.

Stripping. The lithographer's flat, on which the negatives are assembled and taped into position, is a sheet of opaque yellow paper or plastic called a *goldenrod.* Since the goldenrod is opaque, holes, or windows, must be cut into the opaque sheet to permit light to pass through the transparent portions of the negatives. This is the job of the *stripper* who then opaques—paints out with an opaquing fluid—all imperfections. These include razor cuts, pin holes, and shadows cast by pasted copy. When the layout shows line and halftone copy placed very close to each other, or when surprinting and dropouts are specified, separate flats are made for the line and halftone negatives. This makes it possible to "burn" or expose the plate through each of the flats in turn to achieve combination plates. Lines and areas to be tinted are screened directly on the flat by stripping pre-printed shading sheets over the specified portion of the negative (Figure 39).

The Plate. After the plate has been coated with a light-sensitive emulsion, the flat is placed upon it right side up (not turned over as in letterpress), both are set in the vacuum frame and exposed to the arc lamp. The negatives were not turned over because the plate must have a positive or correct reading image. This image will become a mirror image when transferred to the rubber blanket and then once more positive when offset, printed, on the stock. When more than one flat is to be burned on to the same plate, a separate exposure, in exact register, is made of each individual flat. The plate is now developed and washed. The action of the developer removes the emulsion from all unexposed portions of the plate and hardens the emulsion wherever it was exposed to light. The hardened emulsion, the printing image, will now repel water and hold ink while the clear portions, the non-printing areas, will retain water and repel ink. When required, the plate gets a slight etch with acid to achieve better wearing qualities over long press runs (Figure 40).

Multiple Copies. The choice of the press on which a given offset job is to be printed will depend upon the size of the printed piece and the quantity to be run. For long press runs it is often more economical to use a press with a plate size much larger than the layout requires, because several identical copies can then be printed by one plate on one sheet of paper and then cut apart. Multiple copies of the same image can be imposed on the plate automatically by a "step-and-repeat" machine.

Unlike photoengravings, lithography plates are not permanent. They are generally discarded, or resurfaced and recoated for another use, after the press run. The goldenrod flats, however, are retained and stored by the lithographer so additional plates can be made from them when needed.

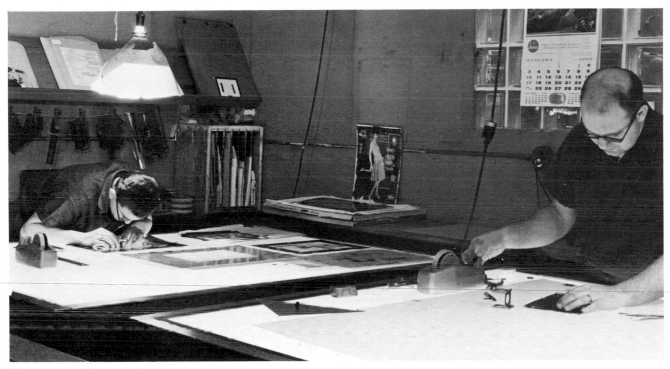

39 Stripping tables in a lithography shop.

a. Setting the camera.

40 Photographs of platemaking
in offset lithography plant.
(NATIONAL LITHOGRAPHER)

b. Copy on the copy board.

c. Stripping negatives into the flat.

d. Opaquing the negatives.

e. Drying the plates.

f. Correcting the plate on the press.

Platemaking For Gravure—
The Intaglio Printing Plate

For letterpress printing on flat-bed presses, we have learned that the plate can be any size up to the maximum dimensions of the bed and that photoengravings are blocked type-high. We have also learned that the lithographic plate, a single sheet of metal wrapped around a cylinder, can be only one size for any given press, regardless of the size of the printing image. In gravure printing, we again have a single plate-size for any one press, but, in this case, the plate is the cylinder and is called the printing cylinder. It is usually copper or, for long press runs, nickel- or chrome-plated.

All gravure copy, line as well as continuous tone, is screened. The halftone screen breaks the image up into tiny dots just as in photoengraving and offset, but here the printed dots are all of equal size. Coarse or fine screens are available, though 150 lines to the inch is the one most commonly used.

The gravure screen is the reverse of the photoengraving screen. Instead of opaque lines on a transparent background, it has transparent lines on an opaque background. This results in an intaglio printing surface formed by tiny wells etched into the plate—incised halftone dots. The wells are all the same diameter; they differ only in depth. It is the depth of each well that determines the amount of ink each will hold. And the amount of ink deposited on the paper determines the tones in gra-vure printing. A dense tone in the original copy will cause deep wells in the printing plate, and deep wells deposit a heavy layer of ink on the paper to reproduce the dense tone in the original copy. Shallow wells deposit less ink for lighter tones.

Again, the first step in making the plate is photographic. But the procedure differs from that used for letterpress and offset. Here, continuous-tone copy is photographed on film that is sensitive to values of gray and therefore records the tonal gradations of the original copy. No halftone screen is used at this stage so the film is a normal, photographic continuous-tone negative. Line copy, however, is photographed on high-contrast film, which records only black and white as in the other processes. After all copy is photographed, the negatives are retouched and corrected where necessary, then assembled as indicated by the layout or mechanical.

This assemblage of negative film is photographed again to produce a continuous-tone positive. Since a positive is the opposite of a negative in value, we now have an image like the original copy except that it is on transparent film instead of paper. The positive film is also retouched.

A medium is used to screen and transfer the image to the printing cylinder. This may be a coating of light-sensitive gelatin on a paper backing, known as carbon tissue, or a silver-sensitized emulsion on a stripping base, called Roto-film. The medium is referred to as the *resist* because it resists the action of acid during etching. It becomes acid resistant through exposure to light. The entire depth of the coating becomes hard, insoluble and acid resistant wherever it is exposed to a very strong light; where lesser intensities of light strike the coating, it becomes insoluble and acid resistant to lesser depths; areas completely shielded from light remain unaffected.

The first step in preparing the resist is to expose it to light through a glass screen in a vacuum frame. This is the first time the halftone screen has been used. Since light could pass only through the transparent lines of the screen, the resist now has hard lines that are insoluble and acid resistant, while the gelatin squares between the lines remain soluble and light sensitive (Figures 41a, b).

The resist is exposed to light once more, but this time through the continuous-tone positive film. The still light-sensitive, water-soluble squares are now affected by the varying intensities of light passing through the film. Some harden completely, others harden to greater or lesser depths, depending on how much light strikes them (Figures 41c, d).

The resist is now wrapped around the copper cylinder with the exposed gelatin face-down. It is developed by revolving the cylinder in hot water, which removes the paper backing and washes away the soluble portions of the gelatin. Varying thicknesses of hard, acid-resistant gelatin remain; the

41 Steps in the production of a gravure (intaglio) printing cylinder.

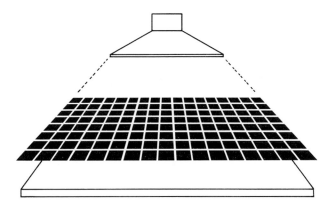

a. Exposure through glass screen.

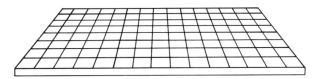

b. Network of acid resistant lines.

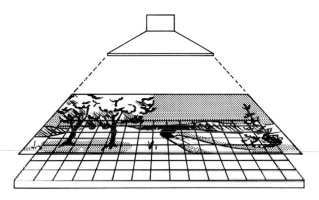

c. Exposure through continuous tone positive.

d. Varying depths of exposed gelatin.

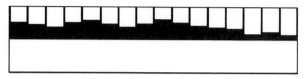

e. Resist with gelatin face down before development.

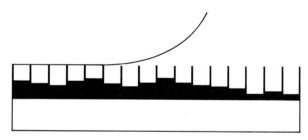

f. Removal of paper backing and soluble gelatin.

g. The etched wells.

h. The inked plate.

lines of the screen, of course, cover the cylinder. Areas that are not to be etched, the pure whites, are painted out with an acid resist (Figures 41e, f).

An etching acid is then applied which penetrates the gelatin and eats into the metal. The acid bites into the plate sooner and deeper where there is less resist, where the film image was denser. The result is the network of etched walls, of the same diameter but varying depths, that form gravure's intaglio printing surface (Figures 41g, h).

Gravure plates are also produced by the Dultgen Process. This process produces wells of varying size as well as varying depth and is used for more sensitive work.

CHAPTER 3

TYPOGRAPHY

42 a. A single letter of foundry type.

b. A line of type cast as a single slug by a
line-casting machine.

c. Lines of individual
Monotype letters.

HAIRLINE — SERIF

COUNTER — STEM

NECK
OR BEARD

SHOULDER

FACE

BODY OR
SHANK

NICK

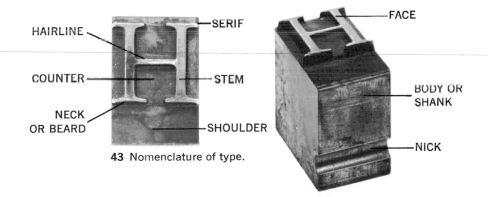

43 Nomenclature of type.

The foregoing chapters have dealt with reproduction processes which should be understood by any artist who may be expected to prepare a mechanical. The professional production artist must be intimately familiar with them.

Since typography and type proofs are basic elements of the mechanical, broad understanding of this subject is desirable. The production artist who understands the mechanics of type and is also able to do *copy casting* is certainly more valuable to his firm and to the team he is a part of. This chapter is intended as a general study of the mechanics of type with specific instructions for copy casting.

We know that metal type is actually a relief printing plate of a single letter or groups of letters (Figure 42), that type can be inked and printed directly in the letterpress process, either as type alone or locked-up and printed in combination with blocked photoengravings. We also know that reproduction proofs, printed from type on a letterpress proof press, become line art to be used in mechanicals for any printing process.

Type sizes are expressed in *points*. A point is an arbitrary unit of measurement approximately one seventy-second of an inch, or 72 points to an inch. The size of type is determined by the number of points in the height of the top side (or face) of the body (Figure 43).

The length of a line of type is measured in *picas*. A pica contains 12 points and there are 6 picas to a

61

linear inch (Figure 44). Only the point system and pica scales should be used in typographic specifications since they do not precisely coincide with the inch scale. There are slightly more than 6 picas to an inch; therefore an inch is slightly less than 72 points.

Space between lines of type is called *leading* and is measured in points. *Lead* refers to the strips of lead placed between type lines to make the spaces. These lead strips are lower than the type and will not print (Figure 45).

Newspapers sell advertising space by the *agate* line. Agate is a type size, approximately 5 points, and there are fourteen agate lines to the inch. The classified sections of most newspapers are set in agate type. An agate line refers to the space occupied by one line of agate type on one column in a

44 a. The pica and inch scales on one ruler.

b. The agate scale on the other side of the same ruler.

Good Sense is, of all things among men, the most equally distributed; for every one thinks himself so abundantly provided with it, that those even who are the most difficult to satisfy in everything else, do not usually desire a larger measure of this quality than they already possess. And in this it is not likely that all are mistaken: the conviction is rather to be held as testi

fying that the power of judging aright and of distinguishing truth from error, which is properly what is called Good Sense or Reason, is by nature equal in all men; and that the diversity of our opinions, consequently, does not arise from some being endowed with a larger share of Reason than others, but solely from this, that we conduct our thoughts along different wa

ys, and do not fix our attention on the same objects. For to be possessed of a vigorous mind is not enough; the prime requisite is rightly to apply it. The greatest minds, as they are capable of the highest excellencies, are open likewise to the greatest aberrations; and those who travel very slowly may yet make far greater progress, provided they keep always to the straight

road, than those who, while they run, forsake it. For myself, I have never fancied my mind to be in any respect more perfec than those of the generality; on the contrary, I have often wished that I were equa to some others in promptitude of though or in clearness and distinctness of imagi ation, or in fulness and readiness of men ory. And besides these, I know of no othe

45 Different leading between lines of the same size type produces different visual effects.

newspaper. A 50-line advertisement, for example, can take several forms: 50 agate lines on one column, 25 agate lines on two columns, etc. Another method of specifying space in a newspaper takes this form: 50/2; this means 50 agate lines on two columns, a total of 100 agate lines. The first number indicates the number of agate lines and the second, after the slash, specifies the column width (Figure 46).

TYPE COMPOSITION

There are two major categories of type composition: metal type and phototype (referred to as "hot" type and "cold" type, respectively). Metal type is composed by hand or by machine. Some metal typesetting processes combine both hand and machine composition to use some advantages of both.

Hand-set type is the most costly typesetting process but it allows greater flexibility in composition. Machine typesetting is faster and relatively inexpensive, but much less flexible.

Foundry Type—Hand Set

Foundry type can be composed into words and lines only by hand setting one letter at a time. The compositor chooses the letters from a type case.

46 Typical newspaper advertising space and its size designation in agate lines and columns.

This is a tray with compartments for all the characters of a particular *font*. Each size and style of type is contained in a pair of type cases (California job case) stored one above the other in a cabinet. The *upper case* holds the capital letters and the *lower case* the small letters. The compositor arranges the letters in their proper sequence in a composing stick and after use redistributes them in the cases (Figures 47, 48).

Machine Type

Complete lines, called *slugs,* can be cast mechanically by the Linotype, Intertype, Ludlow and other line casting equipment (Figure 49). Line casting machines are controlled by a keyboard. Matrices (molds) for each letter in a line, together with spaces, are lowered from a magazine where they are stored, and brought into contact with molten metal from which a casting is made. The casting is a fully composed line of metal type ready for printing. The maximum length of a line cast on most Linotype or Intertype machines is 30 picas. The largest size type that is cast this way is usually 14 point in most type faces (styles). Larger sizes can be accommodated by line casting but it is inconvenient and seldom done. After use, the slugs are melted and the metal re-used. The Ludlow process differs in that matrices are assembled by hand

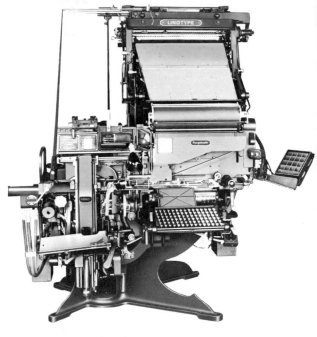

49a The Linotype line-caster.

47 A type case. Each letter is contained in its own compartment for ease of selection. (A.T.A.)

48 The composing stick with hand-assembled foundry type. (A.T.A.)

before the line is cast, no keyboard is involved. Lines of larger type sizes are set and cast this way.

The Monotype machine mechanically casts individual letters one at a time. It also automatically assembles and spaces the letters into words and

49b The Ludlow line casting machine; the matrices are assembled by hand.

49c The Monotype keyboard and casting machine.

lines. The casting portion of the machine is controlled by a hole-punched paper roll which has been set to the required message by the operator at the keyboard. This roll determines which matrices, which letters and spaces, shall be selected and cast. For larger sizes the matrices are assembled by hand. A full range of sizes is cast by the Monotype. Typographers who use this process can cast individual letters and use them as foundry type is used, assembling by hand in a composing stick.

The lines of type, either hand assembled or machine cast, are locked in a chase, in their proper position, for printing or proofing.

Phototype

Phototype composition is the most notable development in typesetting since the advent of linotype in 1878. It is sometimes referred to as "cold type" since there is no molten metal or casting. There is no ink or press involved. The type produced by photocomposition is very sharp and can be greatly enlarged without blurring the edges. Since it is essentially a photographic process using lenses and prisms, infinite variations are possible in sizes and in spacing. Letters can be made to touch or overlap and letterforms can be italicized, extended, condensed, or curved.

Phototypesetting systems vary from simple to highly complex, from equipment that set one let-

50 Phototypesetting systems.
(MERGENTHALER LINOTYPE)

ter at a time to computerized configurations of sophisticated machinery that operate at incredible speeds. Regardless of complexity, a typical phototypesetting system will have the following basic elements: a *keyboard,* a *computer,* and a *photo unit.*

The keyboard, which resembles a normal typewriter, controls the type face, type size, letterspacing, word spacing, and leading or linespacing. The copy is recorded either on tape or on a disc. These can then be used to activate the computer for setting the type, or editing, and can be stored for future use. On most keyboard systems the operator can see what is being typed on a visual display terminal (referred to as "soft" copy) or on a typewritten sheet ("hard" copy).

The computer's functions are determined by its programming (called "software"; the equipment is "hardware"). The computer makes end-of-line decisions such as proper word breaks for hyphenation, or determining the last word on each line in an unjustified column. It stores information such as type instructions, and formating codes. The computer can be programmed for automatic kerning, hanging punctuation, and to adjust letterspacing. It controls the output of the photo unit.

The photo unit is the typesetter. It combines electronic, photographic, and mechanical components to set type at amazing speeds. This is done by flashing a high-intensity light through the type characters that are in negative form and projecting them onto photosensitive film or paper. After the type is set, the paper or film is developed and a proof is made. Paper proofs ("repro" proofs) are used in the preparation of mechanicals by the production artist. If the type is set on film, the typographer or the stripper in the platemaking department makes a film mechanical from which the printing plate is made directly.

COPY CASTING

Instructing the typographer as to type styles, sizes, measures and leading has only one purpose in addition to aesthetic considerations: the type must fit the layout. Starting with the manuscript, the first step in casting copy is to calculate the total number of characters, including punctuation and spaces between words. Count the characters in a line of average length and multiply by the number of lines to arrive at the total number of characters. Elite typewriting has 12 characters to the inch, pica typewriting has 10. This information makes character counting simpler. For example, copy with 30 lines of elite typewriting with a five-inch average line length will have $5 \times 12 \times 30$ or 1800 characters (Figure 51a).

The next step is to refer to the layout for the pica width (length of the line) of type to be set (Figure 51b). Mark off this length on a specimen* of the type face and size to be used and count the number of type characters that fit this measure (Figure 51c). If the type count is 40, then divide the total character count by 40 to determine the number of lines of type necessary to set the manuscript. In our example, 1800 divided by 40 equals 45 lines. Multiply the number of lines by the point size of the type to determine the depth of the complete column of type. Twelve-point type would make a column 45 picas deep: 45 lines $\times$ 12 points. Ten-point type would be 450 points or 37½ picas

deep. Leading between the lines must be counted. Eight-point type with 2-point lead between the lines would also measure 37½ picas deep: $8 + 2$ points $\times$ 45 lines (Figure 51d).

If the copy casting shows that the type, when set, will not fill the depth called for on the layout, then a larger type size can be chosen, more lead can be used between lines, the layout can be changed, or more copy can be written. Conversely, too small a space in the layout would necessitate using smaller type or cutting copy.

Here is another copy casting method which starts with the layout. Measure the pica width of the type line indicated on the layout (Figure 51b). In the desired type face count off, or read from the chart, the number of characters that fit this measure (Figure 51c). Now count the same number of characters on the first line of the manuscript and draw a vertical line down the length of the manuscript at this point. All typewritten lines to the left of the vertical will be a direct line-for-line count of actual typeset lines. Then, count the surplus characters to the right of the vertical and calculate the additional number of type lines necessary to accommodate them (Figure 52).

There are a number of charts, calculators, and books available from typographers and art supply stores, designed to save time and assure accuracy in copy casting.

---

*Type specimen books are available from typographers and type foundries. Charts are also available which indicate how many characters of any type face will fit in any given pica width.

OPERATIONAL SIGNS

- ℛ Delete
- ⌒ Close up; delete space
- ℛ Delete and close up
- # Insert space
- eq # Make space between words equal; make leading between lines equal
- hr # Insert hair space
- ls Letterspace
- ¶ Begin new paragraph
- no ¶ Run paragraphs together
- ☐ Move type one em from left or right

- ⌐ Move right
- ⌐ Move left
- ⌉⌐ Center
- ⊓ Move up
- ⊔ Move down
- = Straighten type; align horizontally
- ‖ Align vertically
- tr Transpose
- sp Spell out
- stet Let it stand
- ⌄ Push down type

TYPOGRAPHICAL SIGNS

- lc Lowercase capital letter
- cap Capitalize lowercase letter
- sc Set in small capitals
- ital Set in italic type
- rom Set in roman type
- bf Set in boldface type
- wf Wrong font; set in correct type
- X Reset broken letter
- ℧ Reverse (type upside down)

PUNCTUATION MARKS

- ⋀ Insert comma
- ⋁ Insert apostrophe (or single quotation mark)
- ⋁ ⋁ Insert quotation marks
- ⊙ Insert period
- ? Insert question mark
- ;/ Insert semicolon
- :/ Insert colon
- |=| Insert hyphen
- ¦M Insert em dash
- ¦N Insert en dash

51b Proofreaders' marks

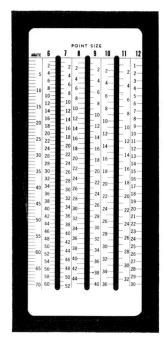

51a Type gauge

52a Typed manuscript marked off for average line length.

52b Layout indicating pica width of type area.

$$\frac{\text{Total character count in MS}}{\text{No. of characters in measured type specimen line}} = \text{No. of type lines}$$

No. of type lines × (point size of type + leading) = Depth of column

51d Calculations for determining depth of type column.

10 Point — Solid

MOST OLD-STYLE TYPES ARE USED EX
tensively in fine bookwork because of their read
ability and because they print well on book pa
per. Advertising designers who wish to give the
ir copy a feeling of age and tradition often use

←————— 16 picas —————→

11 Point — Solid

MOST OLD-STYLE TYPES ARE USED
extensively in fine bookwork because of their
readability and because they print well on
book paper. Advertising designers who wish
to give their copy a feeling of age and tradi

12 Point — Solid

MOST OLD-STYLE TYPES ARE US
ed extensively in fine bookwork because
of their readability and because they pri
nt well on book paper. Advertising design
ers who wish to give their copy a feeling

51c Specimen of desired type style with 16 picas marked off.

$$\frac{1800}{40} = 45$$

$$45 \times (8+2) = 450 \text{ points}$$
$$\text{or } 37\frac{1}{2} \text{ picas}$$

---

40 characters per line

600 characters on this side = 15 additional lines

We are experiencing a new kind of business phenomenon
today.   Competition between product differences is fast dis-
appearing.   The battle has been joined on the verbal/visual
field ... function is common to all.   There are very few manu-
facturing "secrets" today.   The skilled craftsman is a
machine operator.   It is apparent to the small business man
that an "exclusive" product is virtually an impossibility –
that the deciding factor in the purchase of even a small item
is often the consumer's attitude toward the company behind
the product.   This is especially true in fields where a few
companies compete with identical products in an area of limited sales potential.

Every organization with something to sell or something
to say, however small, has an "image" whether they know it or
like it or not.   The consumer sought by small business in its
modest way is the same individual that has been conditioned
by the heavyweights to presume a company's responsibility for
its products – to accept brand names as an indication of reliability.   And what is a "brand" but the given name of a corporate product image?

Consequently, even the bantam business must not exhibit
less concern for the reliability of his firm and product than
the buyer has come to demand.   To establish confidence he
must first identify himself.   Failure to do so properly can
only result in a confused, disorganized image (and there will
be an image in spite of "who needs it?").   It must ultimately
reflect itself in the consumer's attitude.

Many of today's businessmen find their time totally occupied with the day-to-day operation of their enterprises.   The
myriad details that need attending leave little time for the

30 lines + 15 lines

52 Typewritten manuscript with type-line character count marked off and total number
of typeset lines calculated.

JSB
#140
IFT-103
200.
250.
12 X 16
338.70
20-10
200

CHAPTER 4
TOOLS, EQUIPMENT, & MATERIALS

Because the talents and efforts of the production artist are aimed at satisfying the requirements of the reproduction processes, he must be familiar with their principles and understand their limitations. But in order to prepare the art for these processes—to execute a professional mechanical—this understanding must be coupled with ability to use the "tools of the trade" expertly. In other words, the professional production artist must be a competent craftsman if he is to be qualified as a specialist.

The number and variety of tools and equipment intended for use in the commercial art field is virtually endless. They range from complex mechanisms of obscure purpose to the very simple, but necessary razor blade. New products enter the market regularly which are presumably designed to make the artist's work easier and faster, and some do. But there is no substitute for the time-tested tools that are basic to the craft. And an essential requisite for the artist especially the production artist—is to be intimately familiar with these tools, their function, use and care.

As with most manufactured items, there is a wide range of quality and price in art materials. Inferior products, often attractively priced, cannot be expected to perform as well or as long as products of proven quality. In choosing tools to fit his particular needs, student and professional alike should bear in mind that it is usually false economy to buy on the basis of price alone. A good tool, rather than a cheap one that seems "adequate," pays dividends in better service over a longer period of time.

Some instruments are designed for a single, specialized function; many of the more familiar, conventional tools can serve multiple purposes. Outlined here are the basic equipment, tools, and materials required for daily performance.

EQUIPMENT

Drawing Table

The table is the supporting surface upon which you work. Several designs are available—single pedestal, double base, 4 legs—but basically, the table should have a top that can be tilted, raised and lowered. Some can also swivel. The table top is actually a precision-made drawing board, but it is more often used as a support for another board. This preserves the table for permanent use as a piece of furniture. Several boards of different sizes can be used interchangeably, or replaced when necessary, without dismantling the table (Figure 53).

Chair

Any chair will do, of course, but for convenience and comfort, it is best to have one with a swivel seat that raises and lowers. A compensating back support will add to your comfort, an important consideration if you spend many hours working at the board. Casters, another optional convenience, facilitate moving about (Figure 54).

53 Drawing table.

54 Chair with compensating back.

55 Tabouret with drawers and storage bins.

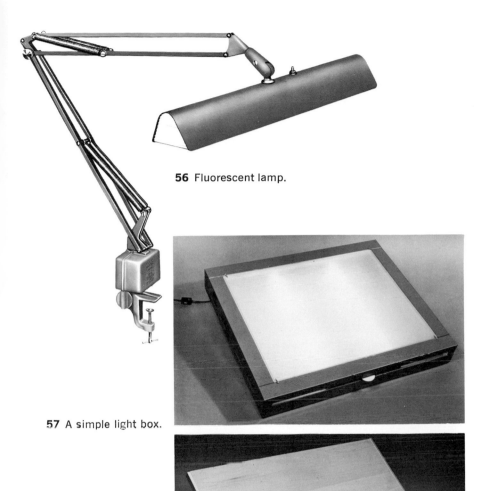

56 Fluorescent lamp.

57 A simple light box.

58 Drawing board with embedded metal edges.

Tabouret

This is an artist's cabinet with drawers for tools, paints, etc., cabinet space for cement jars, spray cans, etc., and vertical bins for pads and papers. The top, sometimes fitted with an additional sliding shelf, is used as a working surface upon which constantly used tools can be kept close at hand (Figure 55).

Lamp

A two-tube, adjustable, fluorescent lamp is probably the most practical type. It remains cool, casts sufficient diffused light and can be adjusted to illuminate any portion of the board at which you are working (Figure 56).

Light Box or Tracing Box

This is simply a box with a frosted glass top illuminated from inside with fluorescent tubes. It is used for tracing through translucent papers and for viewing photographic negatives or color transparencies. Very simple boxes to extremely elaborate pieces of equipment are available in several sizes (Figure 57).

Drawing Board

Drawing boards are usually made of pine or basswood. The essential characteristics of a good board are warp-free construction and perfectly straight edges. Some have metal edges embedded by the manufacturer to ensure straight sides (Figure 58). Drawing boards are available in many sizes.

TOOLS

T-square Guide

If a drawing board edge becomes worn or for some other reason is no longer straight you can correct this condition by attaching a T-square guide—an aluminum guide equipped with clamps, available in lengths to fit any drawing board (Figure 59).

59 T-square guide attached to edge of drawing board.

T-square

The T-square is one of a group of drafting tools you will use regularly in your work. Facility with this tool is essential and can only be developed with practice. The "head" and the "blade" of the T-square are perpendicular to each other; they form a 90° angle on each side of the blade (Figure 60). Holding the head firmly against the left edge of the drawing board enables you to draw horizontal, parallel lines along the top edge of the blade. Slide the T-square down after each stroke, maintaining pressure with your left hand and drawing with your right. Lines are drawn from left to right (Figure 61). Left handed artists either apply the holding pressure with the right hand at the blade end of the T-square or use the right side of the board for the T-square head.

A perfectly smooth edge is essential to the proper functioning of a T-square. Cutting of any kind should never be done against a T-square; use a steel tool for this purpose. An important characteristic of a good, professional T-square is that the blade edges never really touch the working surface. In the wooden T-square, the plastic edges are slightly thinner than the wood so that there is clearance between the work surface, on which the wooden blade rests, and the plastic edges. In the metal T-square both edges of the blade are beveled so that the outermost edge, in effect, clears the work surface by the thickness of the blade. T-squares are available in sizes to match standard drawing boards.

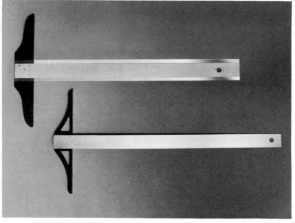

60 A wooden T-square with transparent plastic edge and a stainless-steel T-square.

61 Correct method for using T-square with a drawing board.

62 Triangle and T-square used together to draw perpendicular lines.

Triangle

This is the companion tool to the T-square. The primary function of the triangle is to enable you to draw vertical lines perpendicular to those drawn with the T-square. Never use the T-square on two sides of the drawing board to draw perpendicular lines; a drawing board is rarely square.

Maintaining pressure against the head of the T-square, hold the triangle firmly against the top edge of the blade. Sliding the triangle along the blade makes it possible to draw parallel lines perpendicular to the T-square (Figure 62).

When the vertical side of the triangle is to the left—the normal position for most lines—turn your body so that you draw from left to right, from the T-square, up. When drawing on the extreme right side of the board with the vertical side of the triangle to the right, turn your body in the other direction. This positions you relatively parallel to the vertical side and eliminates any uncomfortable contortions of arm or wrist while permitting normal left to right drawing, in this case, from the top of the triangle down. Turning the triangle on its hypotenuse makes it possible to draw lines at an angle to the T-square. This angle is dependent upon the shape of the triangle you are using: 45°, 45°, 90° or 30°, 60°, 90° (Figure 63). Adjustable triangles are also available; they can be set at any angle. Triangles are manufactured of clear plastic in several sizes. For general board work, the 12 or 14 inch size is the most practical. If you require a triangle for cutting, provide yourself with a steel instrument. Cutting against a plastic edge will soon make it worthless.

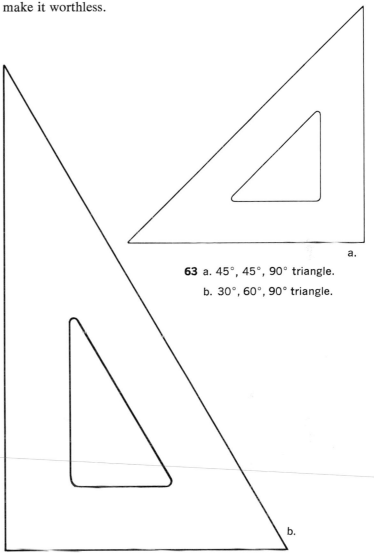

63 a. 45°, 45°, 90° triangle.

b. 30°, 60°, 90° triangle.

French Curve

This tool is also made of transparent plastic and comes in dozens of different shapes and sizes (Figure 64). The French curve is used primarily to draw continuous, smooth curves that are not standard geometric forms. A single, complex, curved line may require the use of several French curves each contributing segments of the line (Figure 65).

To draw a complex curve, first select a portion of the French curve that coincides with a segment of the curve you wish to draw. Draw this segment only. Now select another segment, using the same or another French curve, and draw it coming close to or actually joining the previous section drawn. Continue this way until the line is complete. Any small gaps between line segments that may have been left open can now be filled by choosing proper French curve sections, or, in some cases, freehand.

The same general rule applies here as for the previously described tools. Always draw in the normal left to right direction at the top edge of the instrument. Using the French curve correctly, may require turning the work.

64 Several French curves.

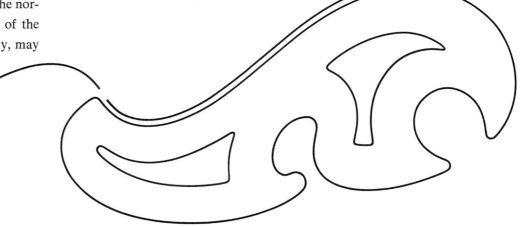

65 A complex curve drawn with the French curve.

Templates

Clear plastic templates are available for a variety of geometric and other common forms in a range of sizes. These forms can be drawn directly using the edge of the stamped-out portions as guides (Figure 66).

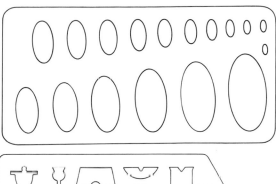

66 Templates for ovals and chemical symbols. A great variety of sizes and subjects are available.

Graphite Pencil

Graphite pencils are used for drawing guide lines, some of which may finally be inked. These lines should be thin and light. Graphite pencils are graded from hard (H through 9H) to soft (HB through 6B). A medium-hard pencil is best suited to our purposes (3H, 4H, or 5H). Be careful not to apply undue pressure. The hard point will gouge the surface and make it difficult to ink the lines. Many artists prefer to use lead holders rather than the conventional pencil. Graphite leads are graded in the same way as pencils and most holders will accommodate any standard lead (Figure 67).

Practice using pencils with the tools we have discussed until you have developed reasonable facility and work with comfort. Draw your lines with a smooth even stroke, always resting your pencil against the top edge of your guiding tool.

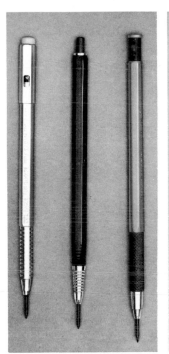

67 Graphite lead-holders and pencils.

Ruling Pen

The ruling pen (Figure 68) is a precision drafting instrument designed to draw lines of constant thickness with any fluid medium such as ink, watercolor, dye, etc. For efficiency, accuracy, and dependability, it is necessary to choose an instrument of good quality with sharp precision-ground blades. The ruling pen is used with a supporting edge such as a T-square, triangle, or French curve—not as a freehand drawing tool. The space between the blades of the pen is adjusted by tightening or loosening the control knob; this determines the thickness of the line to be drawn. Keep the pen clean! Don't allow ink or paint to dry on the blades. Wash and dry

the instrument after each use. Never scrape dried ink off the blades. Encrusted ink can be removed with a rag and water or a commercial pen cleaner. Some pens have blades that snap open or twist apart for more convenient cleaning.

The ruling pen is filled with drawing ink while held in a vertical position, point down and the blades close together. Other media, such as watercolors, can also be used in the ruling pen, but they must first be thinned to the consistency of ink. Use the dropper supplied with the ink bottle to squeeze two or three drops of ink between the blades (Figure 69). When paint is being used, color can be deposited between the blades with the tip of a small

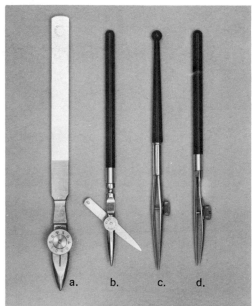

68 a. A pen with a large ink capacity. b. Ruling pen with twist-open device for easy cleaning. c. General purpose ruling pen. d. A ruling pen designed for drawing extremely fine lines.

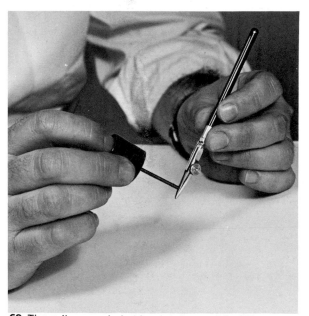

69 The ruling pen is held point-down while filling.

brush. The ink will flow to the tips of the blades and stop; it will not escape unless the blades are extremely far apart. Be sure to remove any ink that has been deposited on the outer surfaces by wiping gently and carefully with a rag. Now adjust for the approximate thickness of line by turning the control knob. Finer adjustments are made after the line has been tested on a piece of scrap paper.

The pen is held with the control knob facing away from the edge of the guide tool. Ink will flow when the pen is drawn along the paper with both blade tips touching with equal light pressure. To draw a line, lean the pen against the top edge of the T-square or other supporting tool so that the point does not touch the juncture of the guiding edge and the paper. This is extremely important, especially when drawing against a triangle or French curve. Touching this critical point will cause the ink to flow out of the pen and spread under the guiding edge (Figure 70). If the pen fails to draw immediately, try starting the flow of ink on a fingertip or fingernail. Tilt the pen slightly to the right and with one smooth even stroke using minimal pressure, slide along the edge of the T-square until your line is drawn. The ink should flow smoothly and evenly without the use of excessive pressure. Turn your wrist at the end of the line so that the pen is smoothly lifted from the surface without resting

 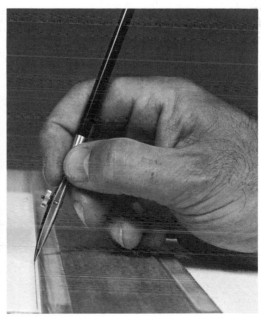

70 a. Drawing a line with a ruling pen and T-square.

b. Proper angle of pen to T-square edge.

on the paper. Notice that the beginning and end of the line are not sharp and square. This is caused by the instrument itself. To avoid rounded ends, draw your line longer than necessary and cut off the excess with white paint (Figure 71).

71 Lines drawn with a ruling pen should be longer than needed. The excess will be covered with white paint to make a square edge.

A ruling pen line is always drawn from left to right. With the T-square, it is a normal, horizontal stroke. When drawing vertical lines, with a triangle against the T-square, it is difficult to rest the pen comfortably against the guiding edge. To correct this, remember to turn your body so that you will be positioned relatively parallel to the line about to be drawn (Figure 72).

In addition to the general-purpose ruling pen, there are others designed for more specific applications: extremely fine lines, large ink supply, swivel-heads for curved lines, "railroad" pens with two sets of blades on one handle for drawing two parallel lines simultaneously, etc. The production artist will find the general-purpose ruling pen entirely adequate for any ink-ruling situation he is likely to encounter.

72 Drawing vertical lines with T-square, triangle and ruling pen.

Compass

This instrument is used to draw circles. One leg is fitted with a needle point and the other with either a graphite holder or a ruling-pen head (Figure 73).

The graphite lead should be sharpened like a chisel by rubbing on sandpaper and the sharp edge turned toward the center. If the outside of the lead is sharpened while it is secured in the compass, the sharp edge will be correctly positioned automatically. Correct positioning assures a sharp edge touching the paper regardless of the radius of the circle drawn (Figure 74). The ruling pen head is filled, used, and cleaned in the same manner as a ruling pen.

Compasses are available in a full range of sizes and several styles. The size of the circle to be drawn determines the size and type of compass to use. The most practical compass is the bow compass, with a screw adjustment for micrometer accuracy. A drop compass is used for extremely small circles. Larger circles are drawn with friction-lock compasses, with or without extensions, and beam compasses. For the larger circles, bend the articulated legs of the compass so that they are almost vertical while drawing.

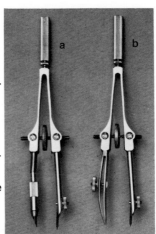

73 a. Small, graphite bow compass.

b. Ink bow compass.

c. Drop compass.

d. Friction compass with extension.

e. Beam compass for large circles.

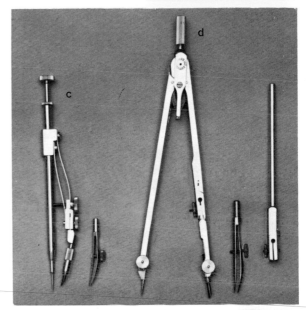

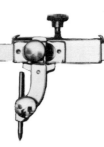

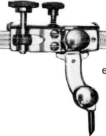

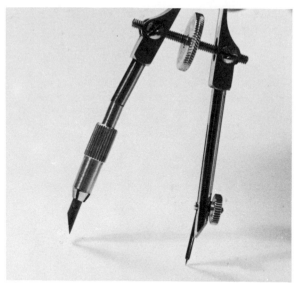

74 Correctly sharpened graphite cylinder in compass.

The compass is held with the thumb and index finger. Locate the center of your circle with the needle without touching the paper with the drawing leg. Draw your circle in a clockwise direction with one, even, twisting motion of your fingers. Don't allow the pen to touch the paper until the compass is in motion, then touch it smoothly and don't remove the drawing leg until you have slightly overlapped your starting point. Lean the compass gently in the direction of turning while drawing the circle; when the circle is completed, lean toward the center to lift the pencil or pen. Don't stop the compass on the paper! Draw circles in one smooth continuous motion, without hesitating or stopping (Figure 75).

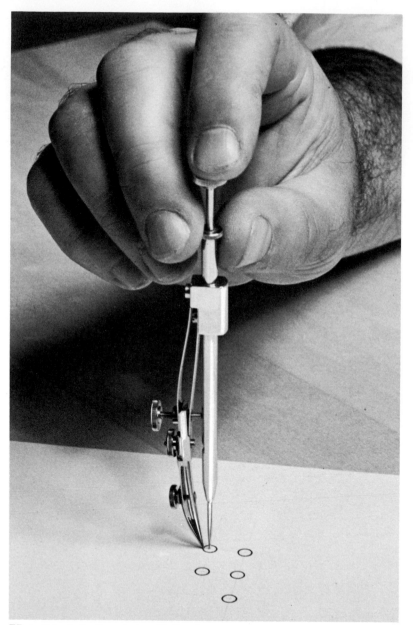

75 a. Drawing a tiny circle with the drop compass.

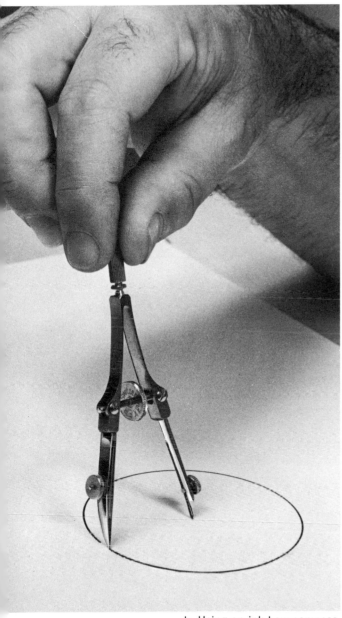

b. Using an ink bow compass.

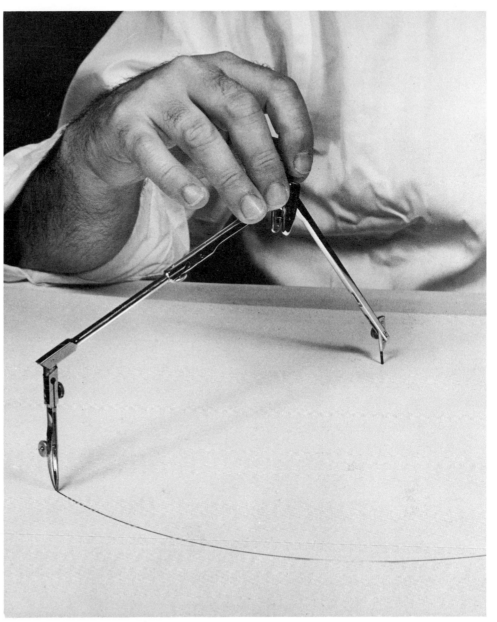

c. Drawing a large circle with a friction compass fitted with an extension arm. Note the articulated legs set perpendicular to the surface.

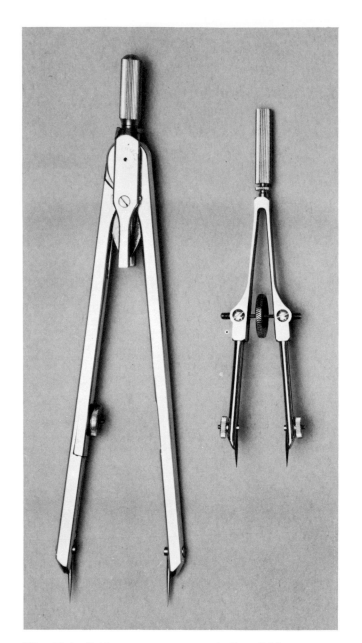

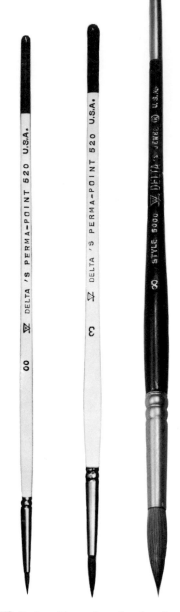

76 a. Plain dividers.　　　　b. Bow dividers.　　　　**77** Technical fountain pen.　　　　**78** Red sable watercolor brushes in various sizes.

Dividers

Dividers are identical to compasses except that both legs are fitted with needles. This is a measuring tool. You can transfer measurements from one surface to another by setting the dividers to a particular length. This same length can now be marked off on any surface by making tiny holes with the divider points. The space between these two holes will be identical to the original measurement, and far more accurate than reading a ruler (Figure 76).

Technical Fountain Pen

Sometimes referred to as "template" pens, these fountain pens use inks exclusively. Paint will clog the instrument. Each pen draws one constant line width and a broad range of widths is available. The point and feed mechanism must be kept clean and moist to ensure smooth, uninterrupted operation.

Technical fountain pens can be used with French curves, ellipse guides, and other templates without danger of ink runout. Long, uninterrupted curved lines can be drawn in any direction. They are also used for freehand drawing (Figure 77).

Brushes

The red sable watercolor brush embodies certain specific features which makes it the most universally used brush in the graphic arts. It maintains a sharp point, carries a full load of ink or paint, and snaps back to its original tapered shape and point after each stroke (Figure 78). It can be manipulated by using just the point; by using the side of the brush, either partially or fully; or by using point and side in one motion. The red sable watercolor brush is extremely versatile. It permits you to paint lines of constant width by using constant pressure on the tip. An increase in pressure will cause more of the body of the brush to be in contact with the paper and result in a wider line. Varying the pressure on the brush will result in an undulating line (Figure 79).

a.

b.

c.

79 Lines drawn with a sable brush and ink. a. Thin line with minimal pressure on point. b. Increased pressure results in a thicker line. c. An undulating line created by varying the pressure as the line is drawn.

In preparing mechanicals, the red sable water-color brush is also used for "cleaning up" with white poster paint, for covering ink errors, cutting sharp ends on inked lines, painting the edges of mounted paper; and with ink, for filling-in between inked lines, for filling-in large areas, etc. There are many other occasions when this brush is the only tool to do a particular job; you will discover its capabilities, and limitations, as you work with it.

The red sable watercolor brush is available in sizes from #000 (very small) to #12 (large). The most useful sizes for the production artist are #1, #3, and #5 or 6.

There is a vast array of brush styles designed for specific uses. Among the more useful for the production artist are lettering brushes (Figure 80), one-strokes (Figure 81), and bristles (Figure 82).

Never allow ink or paint to dry in the brush. This may cause permanent damage to the hairs which can become brittle and break. If the color settles into the heel of the brush, its resiliency will be affected. Brushes should be rinsed frequently while working with them; a jar filled with clean water should always be at hand for this purpose. After use, the brush should be washed with warm water and mild soap until all trace of color is removed, then reshaped and stored. Never permit the brush to lean on the hairs. Taking care of your brushes ensures long, dependable performance.

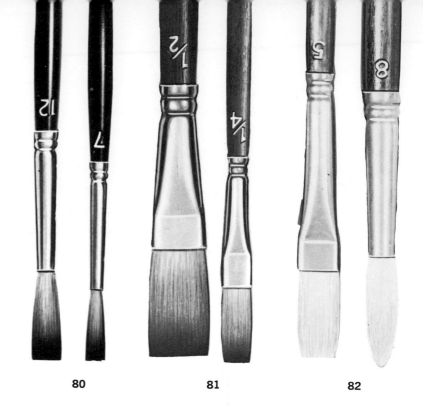

80   **81**   **82**

80 Red sable lettering brushes have round ferrules and straight, even, working edges.

81 Red sable one strokes. These flat brushes come in widths of one-eighth inch to one inch.

82 Bristle brushes.

Litho Crayons and Charcoal

Both litho (grease) crayons and charcoal render extremely dense blacks and are used very often to create art work for reproduction. Each leaves its own characteristic texture and each is used when the specific character of the tool is desired in the art (Figure 83). Because of its wax base, the litho crayon will draw on glossy surfaces such as photo-prints and acetate, and is used to make notations on these surfaces. The marks are easily removed by wiping with a rag.

83 Characteristic textures of charcoal and . . .

litho crayon.

Drawing Pens

The vast array of pen points and pen holders gives the artist a wide choice of styles and sizes. There are pens designed specifically for lettering, others for drawing, still others for general work such as filling-in and touch-up. Some artists prefer the pen to a brush for certain work where the rigidity of the pen may allow more precision and control.

The variety of pens includes every degree of flexibility, from rigid to extremely pliable. They range from delicate hairline points to broad, flat nibs; their shapes are round, square, oval, straight chisel and angled chisel (Figure 84).

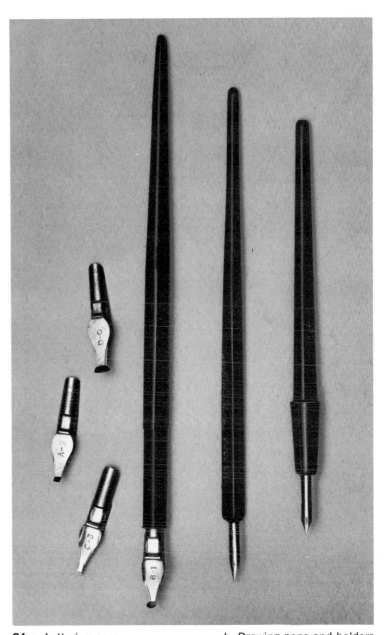

84 a. Lettering pens.　　　b. Drawing pens and holders.

Ruler

The ruler is an essential tool. Three scales are required: inch, pica and agate; these are usually combined on one ruler (Figure 85). An 18-inch steel ruler will fulfill most measuring needs and will be a very useful, straight edge against which to use cutting tools.

Cutting Tools

Most paper cutting is done with an inexpensive, single-edge razor blade, which should be discarded as soon as it dulls.

Straight cuts are made against a metal guide such as a steel T-square or ruler. Use the point of the blade and apply pressure against the metal guiding edge to assure straight, clean cutting (Figure 86).

Another frequently used cutting instrument is the interchangeable knife blade, mounted in a handle (Figure 87). Blades are available in an assortment of shapes and sizes and are generally made of surgical steel. These knives are held like a pencil and the blades can be resharpened to a keen cutting edge. Some handles permit the blade to swivel, to facilitate cutting free-hand curves (Figure 88). Heavy board is cut with a mat knife, which has a thick handle with a large interchangeable blade (Figure 89). A circle cutter is a compass fitted with a cutting blade (Figure 90).

85 Both sides of a steel ruler with inch, pica and agate scales.

Cutting edges can be resharpened on an oil or carborundum stone. Use a drop of oil to lubricate the stone and try to retain the original bevel of the cutting edge.

MATERIALS

Ink

The primary medium used in preparing art for reproduction is drawing ink. This intense black, waterproof ink flows smoothly in a ruling pen, brush, or drawing pen. It adheres to most drawing surfaces and dries very quickly. Red drawing ink is also used occasionally with drafting instruments. Drawing ink should be removed from brushes and tools by rinsing in water immediately after use, while the ink is still wet. An ink solvent may be necessary for the removal of heavy, dried deposits.

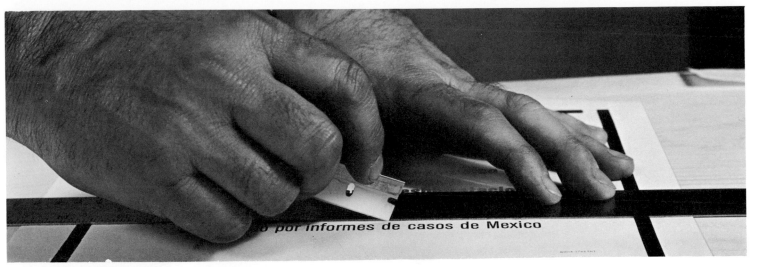

86 Cutting with a single-edge razor blade. The cut is always made on the outside edge of the guide so that a slip would cut into the border rather than the art.

87 Cutting knife with replaceable blade. **88** Swivel knife.

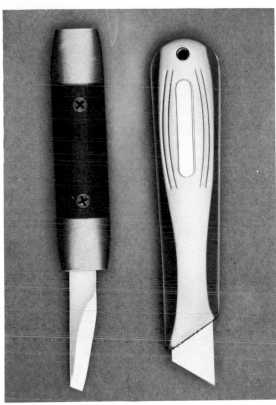

89 Mat knives for cutting heavy board. The blades can be resharpened or replaced as needed.

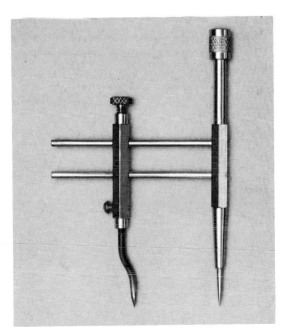

90 Circle Cutter.

Poster Paint

This is an opaque, water paint which can be used with either brushes or drafting instruments. For use in the ruling pen or compass, the paint must be thinned with water to the flowing consistency of ink. Cleaning the tools is easy since the paint dissolves readily in water. White poster paint is used for drawing or painting "white on black," that is, drawing white lines on a black area. It adheres very well to a surface which has been painted with black drawing ink. This characteristic makes the white paint ideal for correcting ink errors. It is also used to "opaque," i.e., to cover imperfections in art work done with drawing ink by simply painting over them with the poster white. This process is not reversible. Drawing ink should not be used over poster paint, because the ink will not adhere; it will crack and chip off. If it is necessary to apply black over an area of white poster paint, use black poster paint. Paint on paint is a good rule to remember—but never ink on paint.

Medium for Slick Surfaces

On occasion, you will need to paint or draw on glazed or slick surfaces such as glossy photo prints or acetate. Drawing ink or poster paint may not adhere properly to these slick materials. A drop or two of medium, added to the ink or paint, will make it possible to work on these glazed surfaces; the paint or ink will hold.

A satisfactory medium is a solution of detergent and water. A commercial medium is available under the trade name Non Crawl.

Illustration Board

This is the surface upon which most art for printing is prepared. Illustration board is cardboard on which a sheet of drawing paper has been mounted. Three surfaces are available: hot pressed (smooth), cold pressed (slight "tooth"), and rough.

The hot pressed boards are best for pen-and-ink work. The smooth surface will offer little resistance to the pen and there is no distinct texture to break the lines. Cold pressed boards are used as a general purpose board and are quite suitable for mechanicals. The toothy surface is excellent for graphite pencil, pastel, crayons, and brush work with paint or ink. The very rough illustration boards are used almost exclusively for fine art and illustration when the texture is an important factor.

A good grade of illustration board will withstand handling and abuse. Erasures can be made without damage to the surface, rubber cement can be rubbed off easily, and thinners can be used without concern. The board is quite rigid and will generally lie flat without warping even after type proofs, photostats, etc. have been mounted over most of its surface.

Overlay Materials

Both vellum and acetate are commonly used for

overlays (see Chapter 7). Each has certain advantages and disadvantages that dictate the conditions of its use. Vellum is heavy translucent tracing paper, available in pads or rolls. It accepts all mediums well—ink, pencil, paint, crayon—and can withstand severe erasure and even scratching with a blade. Other paper can be easily mounted on it. But it should not be used when large areas are to be painted, since the paper will buckle; this distorts the artwork and makes it useless as an overlay. Vellum stretches with changes in humidity. Therefore, it should not be used as overlay material where tight register is called for.

Acetate is available in several thicknesses and is used for its permanence, transparency, and dimensional stability. Ordinary commercial acetate will not accept pencil, ink, or paint. However, specially treated acetate sheets are available to the artist which do take ink and paint. One type has a frosted side which will accept pencil and crayon as well as liquid mediums. Another type is perfectly clear and smooth but is very receptive to ink and paint which flow on smoothly and adhere without cracking, chipping or peeling.

Rubber Cement

Assembly and mounting is so basic a part of preparing art for reproduction, that the word "paste-up" is commonly used to refer to mechanicals. The adhesive used for most of this work is rubber ce-

ment. It is versatile, flexible, and forms an extremely strong bond between paper and paper. A rubber-cement dispenser has an air-tight cap with an adjustable brush (Figure 91). For a permanent bond, apply a thin coat of cement to both surfaces. Allow them to dry and then press together. Any excess cement around the edges of the mounted material can be easily removed by rubbing with the fingers or lifting with a *pick-up*—a ball of dried rubber cement. To achieve a temporary bond, spread the cement on only one surface and mount while the cement is still wet. Material mounted this way is easily moved or removed, but may, in time, be stained by the wet cement.

One Coat Rubber Cement

As its name implies, one coat cement will adhere successfully if only one surface is coated. A smooth, thin coat of cement is applied to the paper to be mounted and allowed to dry. The paper will now adhere to illustration board (or other smooth surface) upon contact. An advantage of one coat is that the coated material can be lifted and repositioned by simply peeling back carefully and remounting. A permanent bond can be achieved by the two coat method described above for rubber cement.

Rubber Cement Thinner

Thinner is used to dilute cement which has thickened in the dispenser. Add just enough thinner to cut the cement to a good flowing consistency. If the cement is too thin, it will lose most of its holding power as the thinner evaporates. To remove paper that has been dry-mounted, i.e., has a permanent bond, soak it with thinner to release the cement. If the paper is not absorbent, lift a corner carefully and apply thinner to the cement. Gently pull and lift the mounted material as the thinner is applied to dissolve the cement (Figure 92).

Other tools and materials, used less frequently and for more specialized purposes, will be discussed when describing the special operations to which they apply.

Other Adhesives

Several other adhesives are available for use in the graphic arts: wax coating, adhesive sheets, adhesive on tape, adhesive sprays, and mounting tissues. Each serves a specific purpose and the technique for use is supplied with the equipment or materials.

Miscellaneous Materials

Masking tape is a self-adhesive, re-usable paper tape to hold your work to the drawing board. *Push pins,* tacks with large push heads, can also be used for the same purpose, but they may get in the way of a sliding T-square or triangle. A *sandpaper block,* strips of sandpaper mounted on a small wooden block, is used to sharpen pencil points to

any desired shape. After repeated use, the top strip of sandpaper is removed, exposing a fresh sheet. *Erasers* will be necessary for removing undesired pencil marks. Special kneaded erasers can be shaped to accommodate any area to be cleaned or erased. A soft *dusting brush* is ideal for brushing eraser rubbings, dust and other particles from the work. For handling small pieces of paper, provide yourself with a pair of *tweezers*. A *water jar* and some rags are necessary for cleaning brushes and tools (Figures 93 and 94).

91 a. Rubber-cement dispenser. The adjustable applicator brush is part of the air-tight cap.

   b. Metal container with cone shaped cap to accommodate the handle of a large flat brush.

92 The spout can is a convenient dispenser for rubber-cement thinner. Here it is used to apply thinner under a corner of cemented paper.

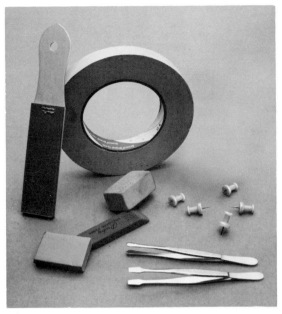

93 Masking tape. Push pins. Sandpaper block. Erasers. Tweezers.

94 Dusting brush and water jar.

95 Various forms of line art.

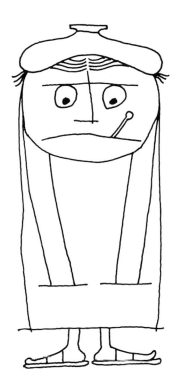

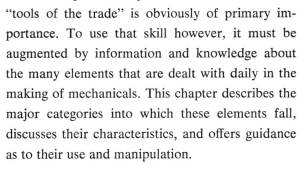

CHAPTER 5

ELEMENTS OF THE MECHANICAL

The development of professional skill with the "tools of the trade" is obviously of primary importance. To use that skill however, it must be augmented by information and knowledge about the many elements that are dealt with daily in the making of mechanicals. This chapter describes the major categories into which these elements fall, discusses their characteristics, and offers guidance as to their use and manipulation.

LINE ART

Drawings

Any drawing that can be reproduced with a line plate or engraving is a line drawing (Figure 95). The tool used may be a pen, a litho or charcoal pencil or a brush. Black ink or paint are proper mediums. Line drawings can also be made with a knife by scraping away ink that has been painted on a special clay-coated white board, called a scratchboard.

Line drawings should be done on a clean, white surface. The medium should be dense black; otherwise all of the drawing may not reproduce because the platemaker's film will not register values of gray that are less than 50 percent of dead black. Drawn lines should not be too fine since they may break or disappear in the platemaking process. Spaces between lines should be wide enough to prevent them from filling in during reproduction. Conversely, any pencil lines or other guide lines that are not intended for reproduction should be

extremely light or completely erased. Guide lines or notations which must remain on the artwork are best done with a light blue pencil since blue does not register on the platemaker's film. Be sure to keep the drawings clean. Dirt marks or rubber cement particles appear black to the camera.

Line drawings are generally executed the actual size of the final reproduction. For more refined reproduction, however, drawings should be somewhat larger than final size, because reducing the size of a drawing during reproduction will minimize its irregularities and defects. Remember that reduction will make the lines, and the spaces between lines, proportionately thinner; so be sure the lines are heavy enough to withstand reduction. Avoid undersized drawings which have to be enlarged. This magnifies imperfections, creating ragged lines and edges.

In drawings done with lithographic crayon or charcoal, only the black marks will reproduce as line copy. Any light-gray lines or soft-gray edges will disappear in reproduction.

Other Line Art

Occasionally, old prints or wood cuts, which are in the public domain, are used as line art. Regardless of the condition of the material used as original copy (usually a photographic print made from a reproduction of an original etching or wood cut) you are nevertheless responsible for good repro-

duction. The prints must be clean; the lines, clear and black. To clean or change some of the lines, use a tool and a medium that will most closely approximate the original technique.

Type proofs, varitype, veloxes, etc., which are all line copy, are discussed later in this chapter. Photostats, which are also line copy, are discussed in the next chapter.

96 Continuous-tone copy reproduced by the halftone process.

CONTINUOUS-TONE ART

Drawings and paintings that have modeling and shading as basic characteristics, are continuous-tone art and must be reproduced by the halftone process. Water color, dyes, graphite, pastel and chalk, tempera, oil, casein are some of the mediums used for making continuous-tone drawings (Figure 96).

The halftone process reproduces every mark made on the drawing. Anything that is discernible to the eye in the original will be seen in the reproduction. Therefore, guidelines must be erased or covered and corrections should be made carefully with the same medium as the original.

The halftone process tends to reduce the visual contrast between values of gray. Drawings intended for halftone reproduction should slightly exaggerate these contrasts. Even greater contrast is necessary in the original art if it is to be reproduced by offset lithography which results in softer reproduction than letterpress printing. More important than the over-all contrast, is the clarity of the detail in each area. Shadow and highlight detail should be a little stronger in the original than is desired in the final reproduction.

The platemaker's film is more sensitive to warm colors than it is to cool colors. Warm grays tend to reproduce darker than the original and cool grays reproduce lighter. The use of both warm and cool grays in the same drawing will make it difficult to anticipate the quality of the reproduction.

Photographs

The most common type of continuous-tone copy is the photographic print. When handling photographs, the following precautions may save many hours of unnecessary corrections either on the copy or in the platemaking process—or both:

1. Don't use paper clips directly on a photoprint. This will cause indentations on the print which might reproduce.

2. Writing on the back of an unmounted print will also cause indentations to appear on the face of the picture. Writing on a tissue over the face of the photograph will do the same damage.

3. Fingerprints, particularly on retouched photographs, must be avoided. The oil from the finger remains on the surface and, though barely visible to the eye, shows up on the platemaker's negative.

4. If a print must be rolled for shipping, do so with the emulsion, the image, on the outside. This will usually prevent cracking; if it doesn't, any small cracks are apt to close up when the print is unrolled but large cracks will ruin the print. It is much safer to ship prints flat, packed between two sheets

97 Mounting a photograph.

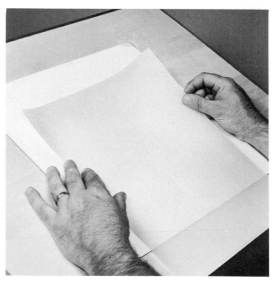

a. Apply rubber cement to both surfaces and allow to dry.

b. Place a sheet of clean tracing paper over the illustration board (it will not adhere to the dry rubber cement). Leave a small strip of the cemented area exposed on top.

c. Place the photograph in position. Check alignment through the tracing paper.

MOUNTING. Before working on a photograph, mount the print on a rigid board, such as illustration board, leaving at least a 2″ border all around for handling and writing notes and specifications. The print is permanently mounted with rubber cement by allowing both surfaces to dry thoroughly before contact. To mount large prints, a sheet of paper is slipped between the photo and the mounting board and slowly withdrawn as the photo is adhered to the board (Figure 97). This technique is also used to mount any large art, paper, or type proof.

Photographic prints can also be dry mounted by the photographer. He uses a sheet of dry adhesive, inserted between the print and the mounting board. The whole assembly is placed in a heated press, which melts the adhesive sheet and presses the print and mounting board together.

Some photographs are slightly wrinkled or wavy. Before mounting, wet the print with water and pat dry with a towel or a lintless blotter. Mount the print while it is still damp using the slip-sheet method. When the print dries, it will shrink and all wrinkles will disappear.

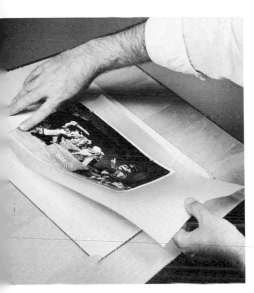

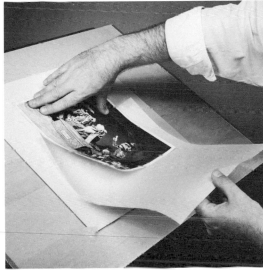

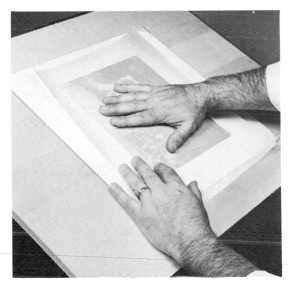

Apply pressure on the top of the photo to achieve a firm bond.

e. Slowly slip out the tracing paper between the photo and the illustration board as you press down and mount the rest of the photograph.

f. Protect surface of photograph with a sheet of tracing paper as it is smoothed out. Remove excess rubber cement from the edges of the mounted photo.

RETOUCHING. Some photographic prints are good enough to be sent unretouched directly to the platemaker for reproduction. Most, however, require a certain amount of retouching to create better copy for the camera.

General retouching on a photographic print is usually done with an airbrush by a retouching artist. The airbrush is a small, precision spray gun; with it the artist can achieve very meticulous, refined work as well as the even spraying of large areas (Figure 98). The retouching artist is a specialist who, in addition to his ability as an artist, must have a good, basic knowledge of reproduction. Retouching is done to improve the print as reproduc-

tion copy, to correct contrasts, remove imperfections, add, emphasize, and eliminate details as required. Yet this must be accomplished without sacrificing the photographic quality of the picture. The matching of color, tonal values, textures, must be exact to produce copy that appears natural. Good retouching is never obvious in the reproduction (Figure 99).

SILHOUETTING. If a photographic subject is to be reproduced in outline form, as a silhouette halftone, the portion of the illustration to be silhouetted must be outlined with opaque white using either white poster paint or retouch white. Since the painted white outline will be the actual outline of the silhouette halftone, it must be accurate. A band about a quarter of an inch wide around the subject is sufficient; it is not necessary to paint out the complete background. Apply only enough paint to render the outline opaque white. A heavy deposit will tend to crack and chip off (Figure 100).

If it is necessary to keep the original print untouched for future use as a square halftone, paint the outline on a clear acetate overlay instead of directly on the print. It is absolutely necessary that the acetate be securely attached to the photograph. A strip of masking tape is used to secure the entire top edge of the acetate sheet to the top border of the mounting board. This prevents the overlay from moving and keeps the silhouette in constant, tight register with the subject.

98 Airbrush.

99 a. Halftone reproduction of an unretouched photographic print.

b. Reproduction of the same print after retouching.

100 a. Photographic print.

b. Subject silhouetted with white paint.

c. Silhouette-halftone of subject.

TYPE PROOFS FOR REPRODUCTION

Proofs from Metal Type

A manuscript is set in type by a typographer in the size, style, and to the layout specified. This type is printed on special proof paper, either dull-coated or glossy, in a proof press. The printed sheet is the *type proof* or *reproduction proof* and is handled as original line copy by the artist preparing the mechanical. The typographer generally supplies four to six copies. The additional copies are retained for reference and as security against mistakes and damage.

Reproduction proofs must be clean, sharp impressions—no broken letters or fuzzy edges. The ink must be opaque black and uniform in over-all color. It must also be mechanically perfect, the lines of type parallel and paragraphs square. Not much can be done about unaligned type except to return the proofs with corrections to the typographer and have him redo and reproof the job. Occasionally, broken letters can be touched up with ink or paint. Be sure the proofs are dry before handling.

Together with the reproduction proofs, the typographer also includes one proof on glassine or onion skin. This transparent proof is used to check the type for size and position against the original sketch or layout.

Phototype Proofs

Since the reproduction proofs from photo typesetting equipment are photographic prints, they are dry (no ink) and can be handled freely without fear of smearing or damage. Simply cement, cut out, and assemble on the mechanical.

VELOX AND LINE CONVERSIONS

These are screened, photographic, paper prints made from continuous-tone copy. It is actually a photographic halftone reproduction of the original subject. The copy is broken up into black halftone dots and the resulting print is used as simple line copy. Veloxes or conversions can be made in any of the standard halftone screens and also in some of the more unusual screen patterns such as lines, concentric circles, and assorted textures (Figure 101, 102, 103).

The lines or dots and the spaces between them must be large enough to be clearly retained on a printing plate. If too fine a screen is used, the print becomes difficult line copy. Veloxes are used primarily for newspaper or other coarse-screen reproduction.

Because the conversion is line copy, you can work directly on it with opaque black or white. Dots can be painted out with opaque white to create highlights (Figure 104) or to silhouette subjects. Black lines can be drawn directly on the copy to combine solid lines or forms with the halftone structure. Several prints can be cut and combined to create a more involved line composite.

101 Horizontal line screen line conversion

102 Mezzo screen line conversion

103 Linen screen line conversion

104a This velox print was made with a 55-line screen.

104b Here, highlights have been painted out on the velox print with opaque white.

ALPHABET SHEETS

These sheets of alphabets and type ornaments, printed on a variety of surfaces in a wide range of styles and sizes are intended for use as line copy. Individual letters can be assembled into words and mounted or adhered to the artwork.

Some alphabets are printed on clear, transparent sheets coated on the reverse side with a wax adhesive and supplied with a protective backing sheet. The letters are sufficiently separated to permit each letter to be cut out easily. After cutting, the letters are peeled off the backing sheet, assembled in their proper sequence, spacing, and position in the art, and burnished in place (Figure 105 a and b). The wax adhesive forms a strong, transparent bond.

Another manufacturer prints letters on individual, ruled strips of paper. The artist assembles the letters into words using the rules as a guide for alignment, tapes the letters together, then mounts the entire assembly.

Transfer type is an alphabet sheet with letters printed on the reverse of a sheet of translucent paper. The entire sheet is manipulated so that the individual letter wanted is correctly positioned on the artwork, then the surface of the paper above the letter is burnished to transfer the ink to the artwork (Figure 105 c and d). Once the letter is transferred it cannot be moved but a mistake can be scratched away with a blade and another letter burnished in its place.

105a Individual letters are cut out and peeled off the paper backing of an alphabet sheet.

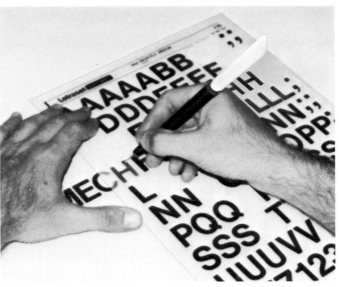

105c Individual letters are positioned and burnished with a dull point instrument.

105b The letters are assembled in their proper position and burnished securely to the board.

105d After each letter is burnished, the sheet is carefully peeled away.

Transfer alphabet sheets are available in black, in white and in a limited range of colors. Their most frequent use is on *comprehensive sketches* where they may replace words and lines normally lettered by hand. They are not intended to replace type and reproduction proofs.

TRANSPARENT, ADHESIVE-BACKED SHEETS OF PATTERNS AND COLORS

An extensive variety of patterns and textures in black, white and colors are available on adhesive backed, transparent sheets. Among the patterns is a group which simulates tint values in fine to coarse halftone screens.

The same type of adhesive backed sheet is also printed in a wide selection of solid colors, both transparent and opaque. In the preparation of art for reproduction, the black sheets and the red sheets are used to create large solid areas.

All of these sheets are used in the same manner. The portion to be used is cut and peeled off the backing paper. It is placed on the artwork in position and burnished. The screened patterns can be placed directly over line work since the transparent base and cut-out marks will not appear in line reproduction. The white patterns and textures are used over black or red areas (Figure 106).

PAPER

Black paper is also frequently used as line art. The paper should be pre-cut to shape and mounted to the artwork with rubber cement. Cut-out black paper will not have as sharp an edge as the adhesive-backed sheets described above, but it has the distinct advantage of being a good drawing surface. You can now draw or paint on the black paper with almost any opaque, white medium.

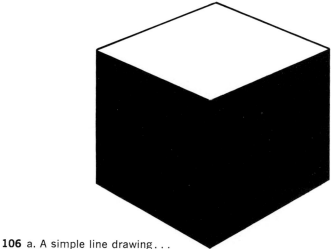

106 a. A simple line drawing...

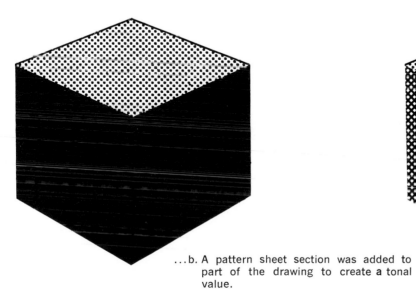

...b. A pattern sheet section was added to part of the drawing to create a tonal value.

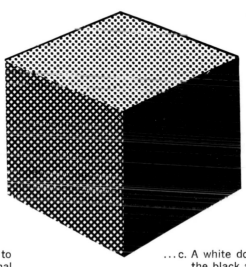

...c. A white dot pattern was burnished over the black area.

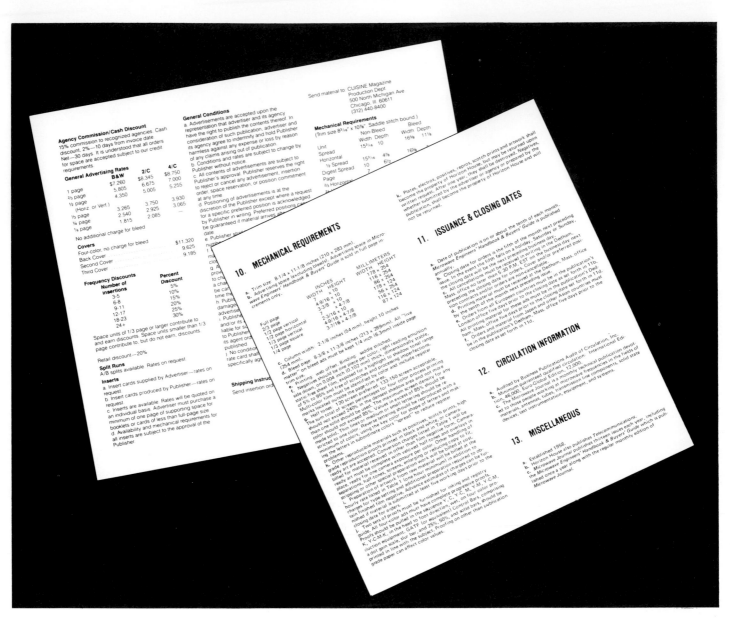

107 Typical rate card for a publication.

CHAPTER 6

THE MECHANICAL— GENERAL INFORMATION

There is no conceivable way in which a text can answer all the questions that arise in production and which must be solved in the mechanical. The production artist's only assurance that he will be able to solve the problems he meets lies in his own sound knowledge of the processes for which mechanicals are prepared and in his intimate familiarity with the proper procedures for preparing the art. Very often the production artist is required to prepare art for reproduction that, of itself, is a creative solution to a production dilemma.

This chapter deals with general information; essential facts and fundamental procedures; practical guides to the making of the mechanical.

The first consideration, before mechanicals or artwork can be prepared, is format: the size, shape and general appearance of the final printed piece.

ADS

Advertisements are pages or portions of pages in newspapers and magazines and are usually called ads. Artwork for such ads must be prepared to meet the *mechanical requirements* — ad sizes, halftone screens, plate and printing specifications, etc.—of the publication in which the ad is to appear. These are clearly stated on the rate card of the publication (Figure 107). They are also available from Standard Rate and Data Service, which lists the requirements of all newspapers and magazines.

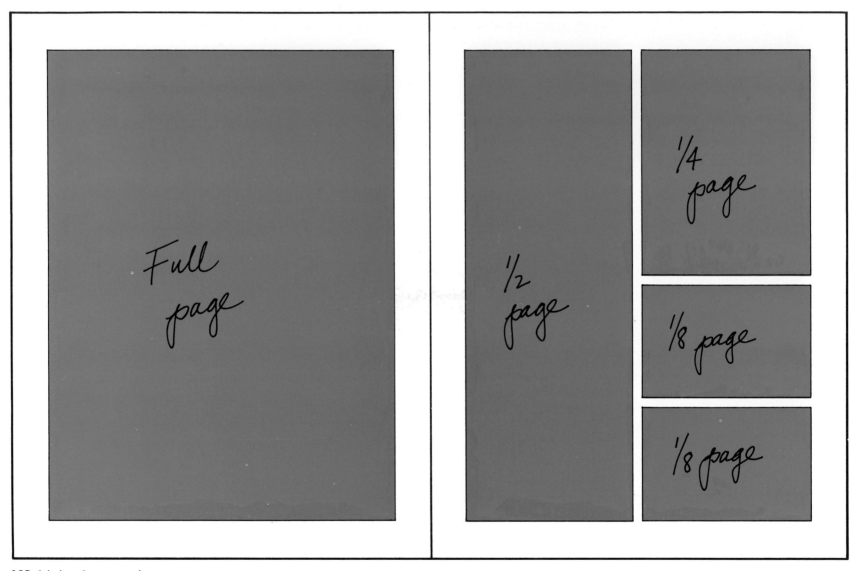

108 Ad sizes in a magazine page.

Newspaper Ads

The size of a newspaper advertisement is designated in inches and columns, or agate lines and columns. The inch or agate-line specification refers to the depth, the number of columns represents the width of the ad. For example, an ad 4 inches on 2 columns is advertising space 4 inches deep and 2 columns wide. Actual column widths vary from newspaper to newspaper; the mechanical requirements include the exact dimension for single columns and multiple columns. Another typical ad-size designation might be 200/4. This is the specification for a newspaper advertisement 200 agate-lines deep by 4 columns wide (see Figure 46).

The complete space allowed for the ad may be used. It is not necessary to allow for a border between ads since the newspaper accounts for between-ad spacing in its designation of columnar widths.

Larger newspaper space is also sold in units of pages or fractions of pages: full page, half page, quarter page, etc. The sizes for these units are also listed in the mechanical requirements.

Magazine Ads

Magazine ad space is designated in fractions of pages or full pages. Borders between ads have been accounted for by the magazine and the full space is available to the advertiser (Figure 108).

ADVERTISING AND PROMOTIONAL PRINTING

Folders, booklets, packaging and other forms of printing do not always take the form of a single, flat sheet of paper. Many require various types of folding, binding and trimming. These mechanical operations are part of the design and are arrived at in the creative, planning stage. Some standard folds are shown in Figure 109.

109 Standard commercial folds.

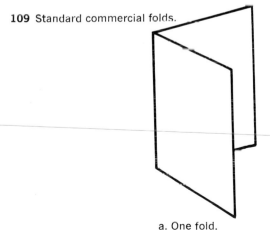
a. One fold.

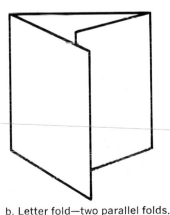
b. Letter fold—two parallel folds.

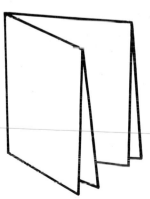
c. French fold—one fold and one right-angle fold.

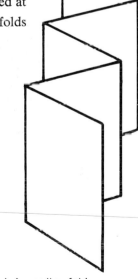
d. Accordion fold— four parallel folds.

Folders

To prepare the mechanical for a folder, open the dummy flat and do the artwork to that shape. Both sides must be prepared so that they fit perfectly when they are *backed up* and folded (Figure 110).

110 a. Dummy of a folder.

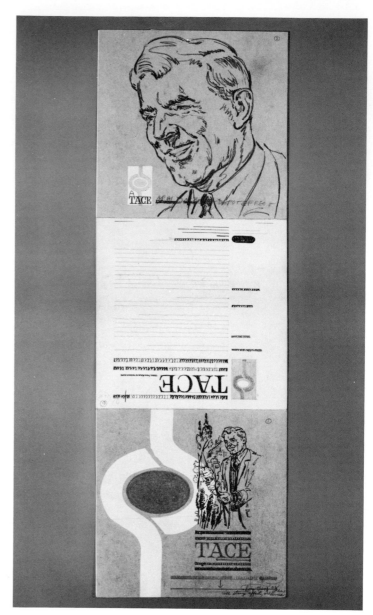

b. The dummy opened flat. The mechanical is prepared for one side...

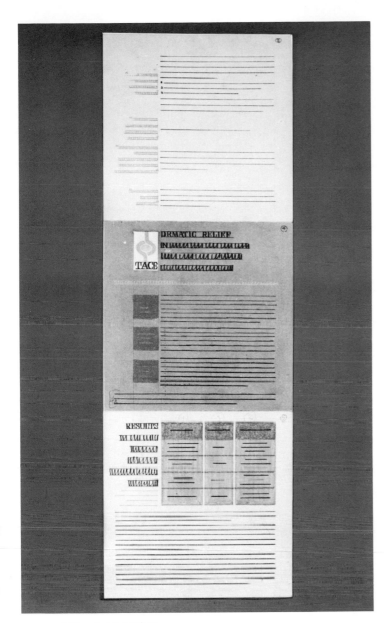

c. ...and then for the other.

Booklets

The mechanical for a multi-page booklet can be prepared two ways: according to the page imposition on the press, or by spreads—facing pages as in a book.

Page impositions are determined by the printer to fit the requirements of his folding equipment. If you are going to prepare art this way, be sure to get the imposition form from the printer before proceeding (Figure 111).

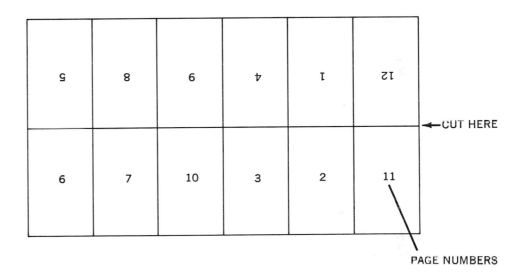

111 Imposition for a 12-page booklet. This imposition will produce two printed copies of the booklet from each sheet of stock. Twelve pages will be printed on one side and 12 pages on the back-up. Each sheet will be cut in half as indicated by the imposition and the halves folded, bound and trimmed.

To prepare the mechanicals for a booklet with the pages imposed as they will appear on the printed sheet before folding and trimming is usually too cumbersome for the artist. The sheet is much too large and controlling the copy as it crosses from page to page is quite difficult and time consuming. The mechanicals for booklets are usually prepared in spreads, facing pages, and the printer arranges the pages in accordance with the imposition.

Dimensional Designs

The preparation of mechanicals for dimensional work—displays, boxes and other packages—is simi-

lar to the procedure used for folders. A model or dummy must be opened flat, as it will be printed, and the artwork prepared for that particular shape (Figure 112).

An exact replica of the flat sheet with all mechanical requirements such as dimensions, cuts, fold, scores and *bleeds,* if any, should be supplied by the printer before the artwork or mechanical is begun. Accurate adherence to the printer's specifications is essential in preparing artwork for dimensional designs. Slight deviations can be disastrous since the unit usually requires not only printing but also scoring, cutting, folding and gluing.

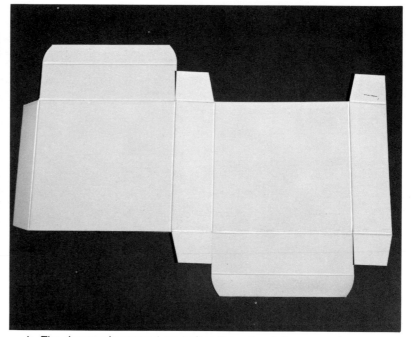

112 a. A dummy of a carton.

. . . b. The dummy is opened up before the artwork is prepared.

PREPARING FOR THE CAMERA

The proper preparation of art for reproduction is directly related to, and controlled by, the procedures involved in camerawork, stripping and platemaking. The mechanical is the prepared artwork placed before the platemaker's camera. Its ultimate purpose is the production of printing plates which involve a minimum amount of work on the part of the platemaker.

Since line and continuous-tone copy must be photographed separately, the line and continuous-tone elements of the mechanical must also be submitted separately.

Line Copy

Line copy is generally drawn or mounted into position on the mechanical in the actual size of its intended reproduction. If all the line elements are in position and actual size, only one photograph is necessary and all stripping has been eliminated.

If the original-art assembly is larger than the intended final reproduction, then all elements mounted on the same board must be in direct proportion to each other and in their correct relative positions. In this way, one photograph can reduce all the elements to the size of the desired reproduction simultaneously, without any stripping.

Indicating the Halftone

Continuous-tone copy is rarely the same size as the planned reproduction. The original copy must usu-

ally be reduced or enlarged by the cameraman and the negative inserted in its proper position by the stripper. The size and position of each halftone must, therefore, be clearly indicated on the mechanical with a distinct guide that will photograph as line copy together with the other line elements on the board. When the negative is developed, this guide enables the stripper to insert the halftone, which is a separate negative, into its precise position. To the stripper, the most practical guide for a halftone of geometric shape—one that can be accurately and easily drawn or duplicated—is a solid form of that shape, drawn on the mechanical in its proper size and position. This form can be drawn with black ink or accurately cut out of black paper and mounted into position. Adhesive-backed colored sheets, in black or red, can also be used by cutting the appropriate shape and burnishing it firmly into place on the mechanical.

This solid form, when photographed, will appear as a transparent area on the line negative; a perfect frame for the stripper to use for positioning the halftone negative (Figure 113).

When it is not practical to use solid forms for indicating halftones, a guide line may be used. A thin, accurately drawn line around the perimeter of the halftone area serves as an adequate guide. This line should be drawn with red ink. Black lines on the mechanical would tend to be confusing since they may take on the character of line artwork. The red guide-line gives the stripper a clean transparent outline on the negative to indicate the position of a halftone. He merely cuts along this line to make a "window," an opening in which the halftone film will fit.

Tinted, or Benday areas are indicated on the mechanical in the same way, either as solid black or red forms, or as red guide lines depending on the particular situation. These areas will be screened to the specified value.

Whatman papers in the popular chromatography grades are cut to special shapes for diverse purposes: multiple strip descending and ascending chromatography; Kawarau horizontal chromatography; continuous electrophoresis; centrifugally accelerated chromatography and electrophoresis. Specify your request and samples will be sent for your evaluation.

Whatman papers in the popular chromatography grades are cut to special shapes for diverse purposes: multiple strip descending and ascending chromatography; Kawarau horizontal chromatography; continuous electrophoresis; centrifugally accelerated chromatography and electrophoresis. Specify your request and samples will be sent for your evaluation.

113 a. A mechanical with a solid black area to indicate the size and position of a square halftone.

b. The photographic negative recorded the solid form as a clear area, a "window," for stripping in the actual halftone negative.

The preceding paragraphs dealt with artwork of a particular nature: line copy that is either the actual size of the reproduction or in direct proportion to the reproduction, and continuous tone art that is to be reproduced as a square halftone or some other easily duplicated shape. But not all line art is actual size, and not all halftones are square.

Photostats

Very often, existing line copy—logotypes and trademarks, drawings, type, etc.—is not the right size, and therefore must be enlarged or reduced before it can be used in the mechanical. Also, the color may be reversed, white on black instead of black on white. Line art can be reversed and the correct size achieved by photostating.

A photostat is a photographic print made directly on paper without an intermediate film negative. The first print, from the original art, is a negative print on paper; the image is a direct reversal in color, white areas are black and black is white. The second print is another direct print on paper, a positive made from the paper-negative first print. The positive second print, of course, brings the color relationship back to that of the original. Reductions or enlargements can be made in both the first and second prints. The first print can be made any size, in one step, from half the size of the original to twice as large. The same limitations apply to the second print, but now the reduction or enlargement limitations are based on the size of the first print,

not on the size of the original copy. This means that a second print, one that duplicates the original art in color, can be made in any size from a 75 percent reduction to a 200 percent enlargement of the original. Any sizes that go beyond these limitations will require additional prints (Figure 114).

114 a. Original line copy for photostating.

b. The first print, a paper negative, was made twice as large as the original art.

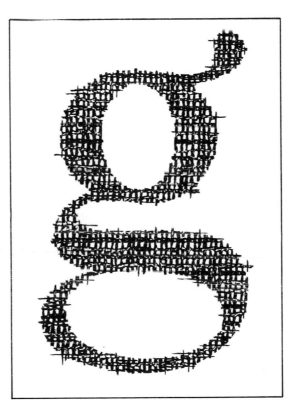

c. The second print, a positive, was made twice as large as the first print.

119

Another very useful feature of the photostat is that the image can be *flopped* to produce a mirror-image of the original copy (Figure 115).

Two basic kinds of photostat paper are used, glossy and matte. The glossy stat is a sharp black-and-white reproduction, ideal for copying line art. Matte stats retain more of the tonal gradations found in continuous-tone art and should be specified when continuous-tone quality is to be retained. When the image on a glossy stat is sharp, clean, and black, the stat can be used as line art in the mechanical. But, when the original line art is rather delicate, extremely fine lines may break or disappear through reduction or reversal by photostat. In such a situation, use the photostat "for position only" and mark it that way (Figure 116). Allow the platemaker to make the reversal or reduction from the original artwork and to strip his negatives into position. This eliminates the inadequate photostat as art.

Matte photostats of continuous-tone art are mounted on the mechanical to indicate the size and position of silhouette halftones (marked "for position only") or any other halftone for which you cannot draw an accurate guide line or solid form. The cameraman uses the mounted stat as a guide for the size of the halftone film negative he is to make from the original art. The stripper will use the stat as a guide for positioning that negative. If, for artistic or practical reasons, you want to use the matte photostat as actual continuous-tone copy,

advise the photostat maker of your intention. He will exercise greater care to retain more of the tonal values of the original. Photostats should be purchased from a professional photostat company which specializes in servicing the needs of the graphic arts.

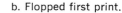

115 a. Original copy.

b. Flopped first print.

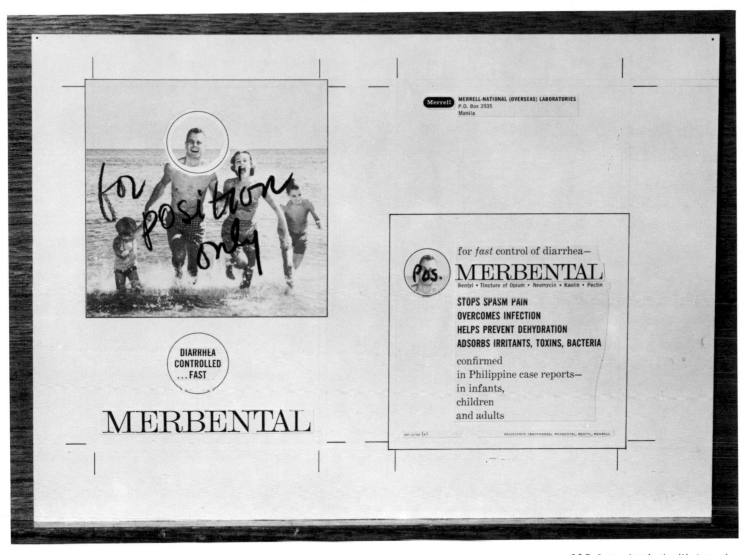

116 A mechanical with two photostats in position, marked "for position only" to indicate that these are not to be used as artwork.

117 Size specification for a photostat.

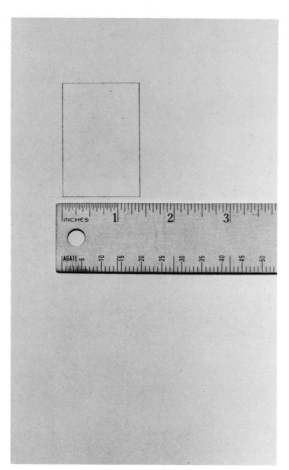

a. Original photograph measures 4 inches across.

b. The desired photostat is to be 1⅜ inches across.

c. The proper specification on the mounting board

ORDERING THE PHOTOSTAT. There are three points of information that must be supplied when ordering a photostat.

1. The size of the final print.
2. The color relationship, whether a first (negative) or second (positive) print. (Specify a flopped image where required.)
3. Type of paper, whether glossy or matte.

The most practical way to specify the final size of a photostat is to measure the original copy and indicate whether it is to be reduced (Figure 117) or enlarged to its final size:

A. 4″ ↓ 1⅜″
B. 2¾″ ↑ 3⅛″

Example A states that a 4-inch image is to be reduced to 1⅜ inches. Example B calls for an enlargement from 2¾ to 3⅛ inches.

The photostat operator sets both measurements on his proportion scale, sets the machine to the indicated percentage, and a photostat is made to the desired size.

Another commonly used method requires two marks drawn on the margin outside the original with the final size indicated between the marks. Figure 118 shows copy marked for a photostat that will measure 3½ inches between the marks. This method requires the photostat operator to measure between the marks on the original and set that measurement on his scale together with the 3½ inches to arrive at an exact percentage. The marks must be parallel and thin to ensure accuracy.

118 Another method of specifying size for a photostat. A T-square and triangle are used to draw accurate marks.

Simple percentage enlargements or reductions of the original can also be indicated as:

A. SS (same size)
B. 2 x Up
C. ½ Off

Example A indicates a photostat the same size as the original, B refers to one that is twice as large as the original, and C requests a photostat one-half the size of the original.

Direct Positive or D.P.

The direct positive is also a print made directly on paper. It differs from the photostat in that the first and only print is a positive. No negatives (or reverse images) are required or available in this process. The only variable is size and ordering D.P.s is a simple matter of specifying the size desired. The direct positive print is a sharp, clean black and white image usable as line copy alone or assembled in a mechanical.

Cropping And Scaling

There are two things peculiar to the reproduction of continuous-tone copy: The original is usually larger than the size of the reproduction; and only a specific portion of the art is generally used for the halftone. Determining the exact section of the original that will be used is called *cropping*.

A simple method for cropping makes use of two right angles cut from opaque paper or board (Figure 119). By manipulating the two angles, the subject to be cropped can be framed in any number of different rectangles until a final determination is made (Figure 120). Temporary crop marks can then be lightly pencilled in the borders. Final crop marks are made in ink, using T-square and triangle (Figure 121).

The crop marks describe the exact area of the artwork intended for the halftone. The platemaker connects these crop marks on his negative to achieve the final square halftone.

In addition to cropping, the artwork must be proportioned or *scaled* to its final reproduction size in order to fit the space allocated for that particular halftone. Cropping and scaling are hand-in-hand operations and the sequence depends upon the starting point.

Working from the sketch or layout, the dimensions of the final halftone reproduction are already predetermined. The relationship of its height to width is the fixed proportion. Any cropping that is done must maintain that proportion.

119 Cropping frames cut out of cardboard.

120 Using cropping frames to crop a photograph and indicating crop marks in pencil.

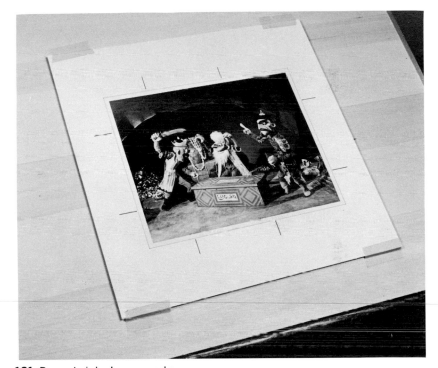

121 Properly inked crop marks.

If the artwork is cropped first—and this may be done for any number of practical and aesthetic considerations during the designing stages—the cropping determines the proportion. The final size of the halftone is scaled down from this fixed ratio.

MECHANICS OF SCALING. The simplest and most direct procedure for scaling artwork is the diagonal-line method. On tracing paper placed over the artwork, draw the rectangle of the cropped image using a T-square and triangle. Now draw a diagonal line connecting two opposite corners. Any size rectangle drawn on the same diagonal, from either corner, will be in direct proportion to the original cropped image (Figure 122).

The diagonal-line method may also be used to scale irregularly shaped (silhouette) halftones. Draw a rectangle, again on tracing paper, completely enclosing the image and, using the method described above, scale the rectangle to the desired size. The scaled rectangle is drawn on the mechanical, in blue pencil, to indicate the outer limits and position of the silhouette halftone (Figure 123). But when the positioning of a silhouette halftone is critical, it is safer to mount a photostat into position on the mechanical. This not only eliminates possible miscalculation, but is also much clearer, graphically, to the platemaker.

122 All rectangles based on the diagonal of the cropped image will be in proportion to the original.

a.

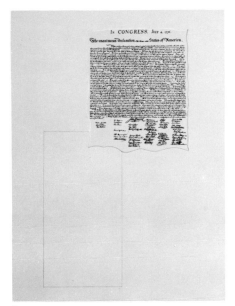

b.

c.

123 a. A silhouetted subject scaled by the diagonal-line method through use of a tissue
overlay.

b. The scaled rectangle should be drawn in
blue pencil in its proper position on the
mechanical.

c. Reproduction.

A simple proportion formula can be used to determine scaled dimensions mathematically:

$$a/b = c/d \text{ or } ad = bc$$
$$12d = 9(4)$$
$$d = \frac{36}{12} = 3$$

The dimensions of the original are known (a,b). One of the dimensions of the final image is established to suit the artwork (c or d). The unknown dimension is determined by formula (Figure 124).

A number of slide rules and proportion calculators have been designed to solve proportioning and scaling problems through a simple manipulation of two known dimensions. The answers are read directly on the instrument and the adjustments can be made rapidly. One ratio setting on a propor-

tion calculator provides correct answers for scaling both up and down in a virtually limitless number of dimensions (Figure 125).

More elaborate mechanical tools and machines are available to fulfill the same function. An adjustable cropping frame can be set to any rectangle and then opened and closed to expose other rectangles of the same proportion (Figure 126). Proportional dividers with calibrated scales can be set to a particular ratio and used to mark off any dimension to that proportion (Figure 127). The pantograph is a device which draws a traced image in direct proportion to the original to any predetermined size (Figure 128). Various projection machines can throw an image from the original artwork directly on to a drawing surface in any size desired (Figure 129).

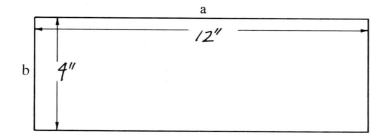

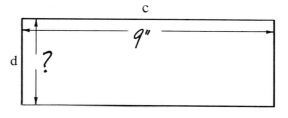

124 Scaling can be done by formula with three known dimensions: the height and width of the original, and either the height or width of the desired size.

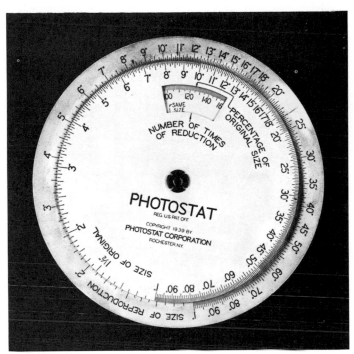

125 Typical proportion calculator.

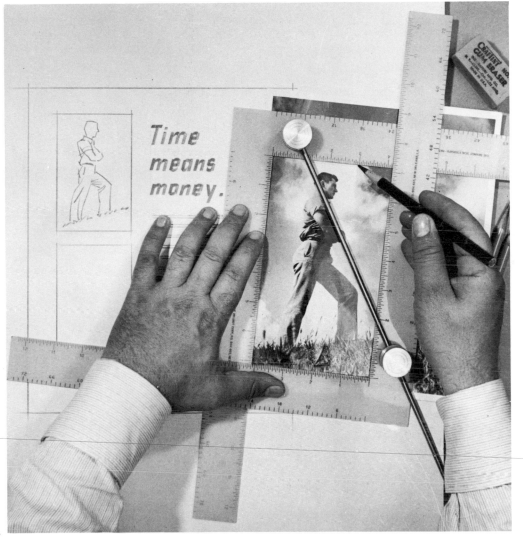

126 Adjustable cropping frame.

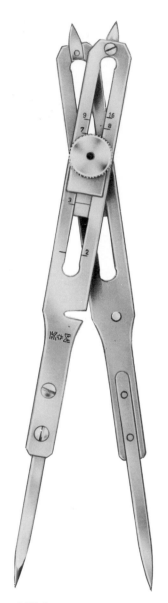

127 Proportional dividers.

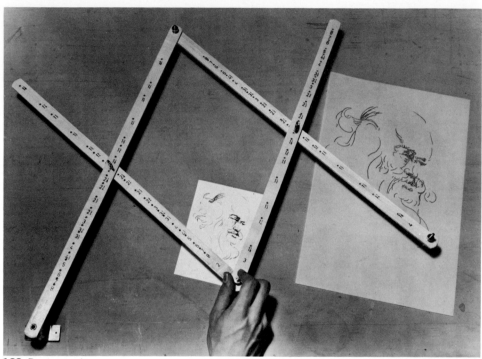

128 Pantograph.

129 Projection machines.

ELEMENTARY PROCEDURES
FOR THE MECHANICAL

The mechanical is usually prepared on single-thick illustration board, large enough to allow at least a 2-inch border around the working area. The border will be used for notations and specifications and will help keep the artwork clean by providing room for handling.

Planning

Begin by outlining the working area lightly with a hard pencil. Draw light, pencil guide-lines for the exact position of all the elements which are to be part of the mechanical — type, drawings, photographs, etc. These can be traced or accurately measured from the layout. The pencil lines are merely guides for your own purposes. They should not be dark enough to record on the platemaker's negative. To show the outer extremities of the sheet, place trim marks in each corner.* These are short, thin lines drawn outside the working area with a ruling pen, T-square and triangle. They indicate the full size of the printed piece, including borders, and will be used as trimming guides after the job has been printed. Folds, if any, are indicated with broken red lines outside the working area. Cuts of all kinds, aside from normal trim, are specified with thin, accurately drawn, red ink lines. If the cut is external, such as a corner cut, use red trim marks in the proper direction outside the working area. Internal cuts, or hole punching are shown with complete outlines of the cut. This outline is used as actual artwork for making the cutting die and should be sharp and clean (Figure 130).

Assembly

After all the pencil guide-lines are drawn, proceed to mount, or draw, all the elements in their proper positions—type proofs, photostats, drawings, ink guide-lines, solid forms, etc. Almost all mechanicals contain reproduction proofs of paragraphs or columns of type as line copy. The proofs must be mounted so that the type is square—aligned with the other material on the mechanical. Draw the pencil guide lines, with T-square and triangle, so that they cross and go beyond the corners. Now draw light-blue pencil lines on the type proof, also with T-square and triangle, from the top and bottom type lines out to the edge of the cut out type section. Use the type body for alignment, not the descenders or ascenders which may vary in size. The cemented type proof can now be placed in position, using the pencil lines as guides, and checked for accuracy with the T-square and triangle (Figure 131). All excess rubber cement should be removed and any dark guide-lines erased. Shadows cast by the edges of the mounted elements are sometimes recorded by the camera as thin black lines. A good precaution is to paint these edges with opaque white poster paint.

Bleed

If any part of the printed image is to run off the edge of the trimmed sheet, it is called a bleed. To ensure complete coverage to the bleed edge, the artwork must run at least one-eighth of an inch beyond the trim marks. This excess will be cut off when the printed sheet is trimmed. Without this allowance for bleed, a white edge might remain (Figure 132).

*The photoengraver will only be concerned with the printing plate area, but the lithography or gravure shop must have the full sheet size indicated since they are usually both platemaker and printer.

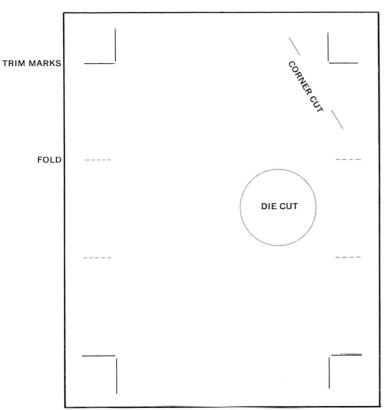

TRIM MARKS

FOLD

CORNER CUT

DIE CUT

130 Marks on the mechanical to indicate trim, folds and die cuts.

132 Proper preparation of artwork for bleed. A closeup of a corner is shown. The artwork will bleed off the left side and top of the sheet.

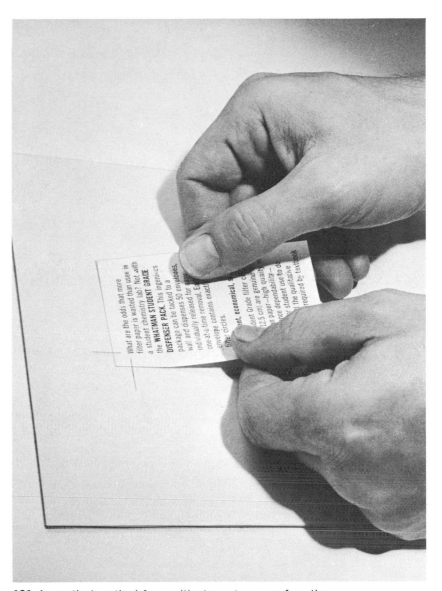

131 A practical method for positioning a type proof on the mechanical.

Specifications

The next step is to mark all the specifications with light-blue pencil. Specifications for tint percentage, die cut, fold, square halftone, etc., should be directed to the appropriate area, element, or guideline with an arrow. If a photostat is used for a halftone indication it should be clearly marked "for position only". All halftone indications should be keyed to the original artwork with an identifying letter.

After all work is done, the mechanical is flapped with a sheet of tracing paper, which may be used for further notations and specifications. The flap may also be used for indicating changes and corrections without marking the actual artwork. The completed mechanical is then flapped with heavy paper to protect it from damage in handling (Figure 133).

In letterpress printing, mechanicals for the entire printed image are not always required. When the type matter—text, headlines, captions, etc.—is to be printed directly from metal type, photoengravings are made of the illustrative material only.

133 A finished mechanical flapped with tracing paper and a heavy protective paper.

134 Both are mounted to the back with rubber cement.

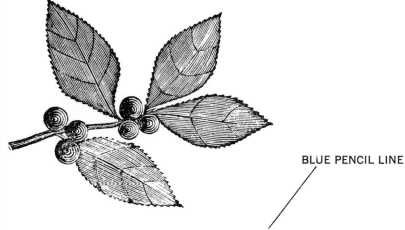

BLUE PENCIL LINE

SALE

*s/s line plate —
cut apart & block separately*

134 Artwork prepared for a photoengraver. The specifications call for a line plate to be made and the elements to be cut apart.

135

CHAPTER 7

THE MECHANICAL: ONE-COLOR PRINTING

Preparing artwork for reproduction is not always the straightforward job of simply mounting line copy and indicating halftones. More often than not, it will involve combinations of line and halftone which are more complicated. Line may overlap halftone as in a surprint or dropout, line may touch halftone, or halftone and tinted areas may touch each other, etc. There will probably be more than one correct way to prepare the artwork for any of these combinations; the choice will depend on speed, accuracy and cost. Certain operations are done more quickly by the artist than by the stripper and vice versa. Many situations require the photo-mechanical accuracy of the camera as opposed to the possible human error in handmade mechanicals even though plate costs increase as you leave more and more work to the platemaker.

Combinations

The basic combinations can generally be handled directly on the illustration board along with the simpler elements of the mechanical. Because indications for halftones or screened areas are guides and not original art, portions of guide lines, solid forms, or photostats may be covered providing this does not make it impossible or unduly difficult for the platemaker to complete the halftone shape.

The preparation of a typical surprint (black line on a screened background) and a dropout (white line on a screened background) can be discussed simultaneously since the art preparation for each is identical; the only difference is in the specification. The type proof covers a portion of the solid form in Figure 135 and covers part of the photostat in Figure 136. The form, however, is easily completed by the stripper and the photostat is sufficiently exposed to function as an accurate guide for the size and position of the silhouette halftone. Line and halftone combinations may be prepared directly on the illustration board, regardless of the complexity of the combination, provided that the positioning of the artwork permits the camera to record enough for the stripper to understand and use (Figure 137).

135 Preparation for surprint. Above: The solid form indicates the exact size and position of the square halftone. The type proof is cemented over the form. Note the handwritten instructions to the stripper. At left is original photograph properly cropped.
Below: The printed result.

136 Preparation for surprint. Above: The photostat indicates the exact size and position of the silhouette halftone. The type proof is mounted over the stat.
Below: The printed result.

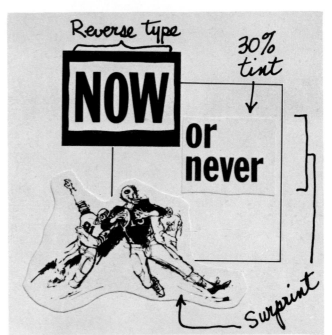

137 Preparation for surprint. Above: A red guide-line is used to describe the tint (or Benday) panel. A proof of the type to be surprinted entirely within the panel is pasted inside the guide lines. The black rectangle is drawn, or mounted, directly over the guide line and the type proof to be reversed is pasted over, but well within, the rectangle. A photostat of the line drawing is cemented in the exact position covering as little of the guide line as possible. Note the very precise specifications which tell the stripper exactly what is to be done.
Below: The printed result.

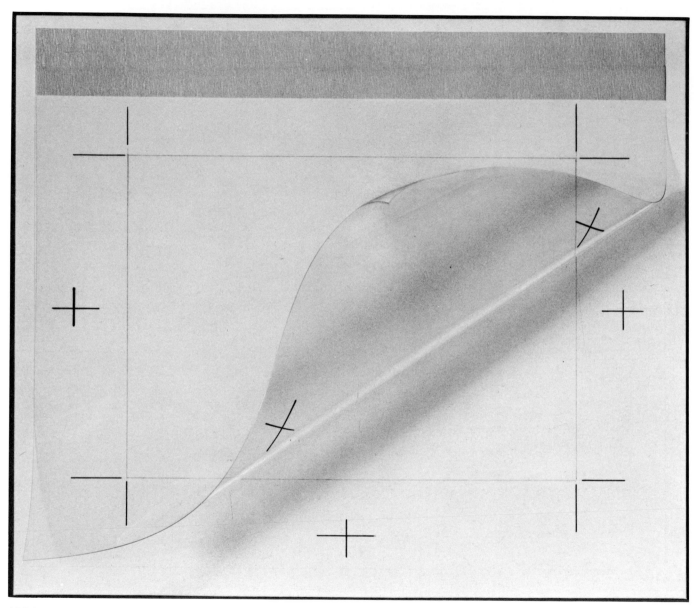

138 Transparent overlay. The overlay is taped securely to the illustration board and register marks are drawn accurately on both surfaces.

Overlays

It is sometimes impossible to prepare all the art for a combination plate directly on the same board. The proper execution of such a mechanical will require the use of an *overlay*. The overlay is usually a sheet of transparent acetate on which either the line copy or the guides for the screened material are positioned. It is extremely important that the overlay and the illustration board be in perfect register. Therefore, register marks must be placed on both surfaces before any work is done on an overlay (Figure 138). The simplest register mark is a cross drawn with the ruling pen, T-square and triangle. One mark is drawn on each side of the illustration board. One edge of the overlay is taped to the board, generally at the top, and register marks are drawn on the overlay directly over those on the illustration board. The overlay can then always be positioned accurately, even if moved, by simply realigning the register marks. The platemaker will have the same register marks recorded on his negatives to guide him in stripping. Register marks printed on rolls of transparent tape are available at art materials stores (Figure 139).

139 Register marks preprinted on transparent tape.

Note: For purposes of clearly understanding the following illustrations of mechanicals, overlays will always be shown separated from their boards instead of directly over them.

Figures 140 and 141 are examples of combinations which require overlays for the preparation of the art. In Figure 140, the type proof would completely block out the photostat which positions the silhouette halftone if both were mounted directly on the board. In Figure 141 a solid form on the same board as the art would cover some of the line art completely; and if red guide-lines indicating the screened panel were drawn directly on the art, it would be extremely difficult for the platemaker to separate the two elements. Both examples clearly call for overlays.

Typical Problems

Every problem in the preparation of art for combinations should be carefully analyzed to facilitate stripping and platemaking. The art should be prepared so that the desired results are obvious and directly achievable. Under extraordinary circumstances, which may go beyond your knowledge of the stripping and platemaking processes, consult the platemaker. His experience is always at the artist's disposal and his advice can prove invaluable in time and money saved.

Each of the following examples illustrates and analyzes a typical situation. Together they cover many of the most common circumstances in the execution of simple mechanicals. These basic procedures, coupled with a knowledge of stripping and platemaking, will enable the production artist to

140 To prepare a mechanical for this result....

141 To prepare a mechanical for this result....

a.
This is wrong. When the surprinting lines are drawn directly on the solid form indicating the tinted area, they disappear on the platemaker's negative since red and black photograph alike.

b.
This is wrong. When the surprinting lines are drawn directly on the red guide-line, the camera will record all these lines on the negative. This would still necessitate two negatives and, in addition, the stripper would have to eliminate by hand the guide lines for the tinted area from one negative and the surprint lines from the other. This can never result in a perfect job—and it is costly and time-consuming.

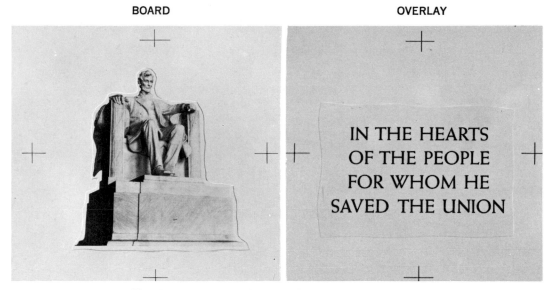

This is wrong. The type proof covers too much of the photostat. It is impossible for the stripper to use the stat to position the silhouette halftone.

This is correct. The photostat is pasted on the board. The type proof is pasted on an overlay which has been registered to the board. The cameraman can now photograph each separately (as shown above) and the stripper will have no difficulty in assembling the negatives. Remember, at least two negatives are always required for a combination plate.

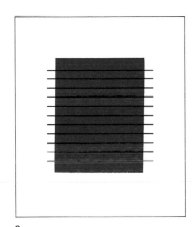

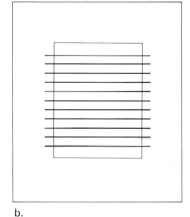

a.   b.

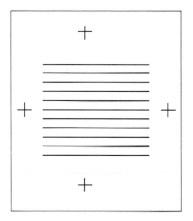

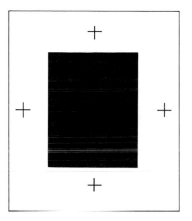

This is correct. The surprint lines have been drawn on the board. The solid form for the tinted area is drawn, or mounted, on an overlay registered to the board. Both elements can now be photographed separately by the cameraman with assured accuracy.

143

determine the best procedure for solving most mechanical problems.

Figure 142 is a simple line-art assembly, all the elements, in actual size, are positioned in their proper places. The type proof is cemented with rubber cement. If the original line drawing of the tree is not drawn directly on the illustration board, a positive photostat (second print) of the art is cemented into position. The black panel is drawn with black ink and a negative photostat (first print) is mounted within it. The edges of the negative photostat should be inked with black to prevent the camera from recording the cut edges. If the platemaker is to make the reversal (Figure 143) positive art (black on white) is mounted within the inked panel, filled in as close to the lettering as is practical, but leaving a ragged edge, and specified as a "reverse".

Figure 144 includes two halftones, one square and one silhouette. The type and line art are handled as described above. A solid form is drawn in black to position the square halftone, which is to be cropped and enlarged. The form could just as well have been cut out of black paper and mounted, or out of black or red adhesive-backed sheets and burnished into place.

The original photograph for the square halftone is cropped, scaled and keyed to the solid form by using the same key letter for each one. A matte photostat is cemented into place to indicate the size and position of the silhouette halftone. The original photograph is silhouetted and both original photographs are sent to the platemaker along with the mechanical.

The new problem introduced in Figures 145 and 146 is the surprint. These figures show two correct methods for preparing the same copy. Figure 145 utilizes an overlay and separates the screened areas from the line material. In Figure 146, all elements are on the illustration board and red guide-lines are used. Notice how carefully the details are specified to the platemaker.

Figure 147 shows line art touching the perimeter of a square halftone which, in turn, touches, butts, a black panel. The type surprints the halftone and reverses in the black panel. Though the platemaking is somewhat involved, the preparation of the art is surprisingly simple (Figure 148). The square halftone, in this case, is indicated with a blue outline which does not photograph so the line art can be drawn beyond the halftone guide. The stripper will trim the line-art negative flush with the halftone negative to achieve a perfect butt. The type is either mounted directly on the illustration board or on an overlay. The written specifications give the platemaker complete instructions. If an overlay is used for the line art (Figure 149) then a red guide is used for the square halftone indication.

been developed to the
and dry in the atmos-
described. If the sep-
arated compounds are colored, the plates are ready
for examination. If the separated compounds are
colorless, the plates may be examined under ultra-
violet light; alternatively, and more usually, color
may be developed by applying a coloring agent with

E-S abcdefghijklmnopqrstuvwxyz

142 Above: The completed assembly of line art
for the reproduction at the right. The type
proofs and the photostats are mounted in
their exact positions.

been developed to the
and dry in the atmos-
described. If the sep-
arated compounds are colored, the plates are ready
for examination. If the separated compounds are
colorless, the plates may be examined under ultra-
violet light; alternatively, and more usually, color
may be developed by applying a coloring agent with

E-S abcdefghijklmnopqrstuvwxyz

Reverse Type

143 An alternate method for preparing the reverse panel. The platemaker will reverse the
type to create the desired result.

INDEPENDENCE

To make a key line, a normal black and white mechanical is prepared on illustration board for the most involved color, usually black. Each of the other colors is then accurately outlined with red ink guide-lines (key lines) directly on the board. The color separation is indicated to the platemaker on a tissue flap by using colored pencils (Figure 157). Working on the tissue flap—not on the board!—each different color area is filled in with a different colored pencil. Exact ink-color swatches are still necessary for the printer. These should be mounted on the illustration board and keyed by name to the colored pencils used on the tissue. A color sketch or dummy should be included with the artwork as further reference for the color separation.

The cameraman will photograph the entire key-line mechanical as many times as there are colors to be printed. This results in a separate negative for each color. On each negative, the stripper will opaque, block out, all the guide lines and art ele-

144 Line plus halftones. Facing page: Complete artwork for this advertisement includes the mechanical and two photographs. Opaque white paint was used to silhouette the original photograph of the building. Crop marks on the photograph of the aerial view are drawn carefully with black ink. All the elements on the mechanical are accurately cemented in position.

Notes to the platemaker, which are not to photograph, are written in light blue pencil. "Position only" is written over the photostat with a red or black litho crayon to ensure use of the original reproduction copy.

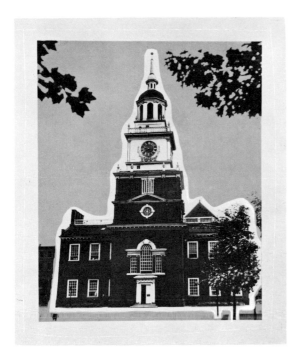

Silhouette H.T.

Square H.T.

INDEPENDENCE

To make a key line, a normal black and white mechanical is prepared on illustration board for the most involved color, usually black. Each of the other colors is then accurately outlined with red ink guide-lines (key lines) directly on the board. The color separation is indicated to the platemaker on a tissue flap by using colored pencils (Figure 157). Working on the tissue flap—not on the board—each different color area is filled in with a different colored pencil. Exact ink-color swatches are still necessary for the printer. These should be mounted on the illustration board and keyed by name to the colored pencils used on the tissue. A color sketch or dummy should be included with the artwork as further reference for the color separation.

The cameraman will photograph the entire key-line mechanical as many times as there are colors to be printed. This results in a separate negative for each color. On each negative, the stripper will opaque, block out, all the guide lines and art ele-

147

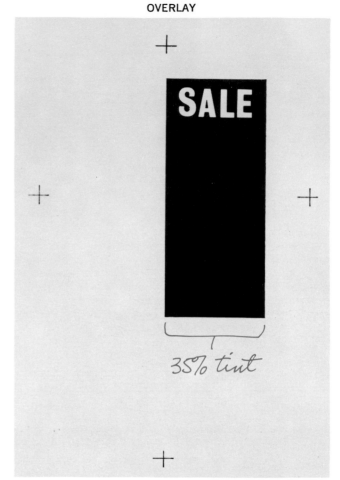

145 Preparation for surprint and dropout. A completely separated mechanical to provide the platemaker with the most direct and economical art. All line art, which is not to be screened, has been mounted in position on the board. This will give the stripper a single line negative. The overlay contains a black panel with a first-print photostat of the type; the panel is specified for screening. The overlay will give the stripper a second, complete, line negative which, when screened, will achieve a dropout effect. This is not a true dropout. It is simply screened line copy accomplished on the one negative. To achieve the dropout specified on the board, both negatives must be used.

146 To achieve the same results with a one-board mechanical, all the elements are mounted, in position, on the board. The area to be screened is simply outlined with a red guide line. Note the specifications to the platemaker. The board will be photographed twice resulting in two identical negatives. The stripper blocks out and opaques the unnecessary (conflicting) elements on each negative to create the same two negatives that were achieved in Fig. 145.

Reproduction

Day and Night

Few faces possess the utility value of Bookman for advertising typography and commercial printing. It is exceptionally legible, prints well on antique, smooth finished and coated papers, and has no annoying mannerisms to distract the reader or become monotonous and tiresome by continued use. Bookman, too, is at home with practically any angle of display face. Its

TELEPHONE

147 Two ways to achieve the above reproduction....

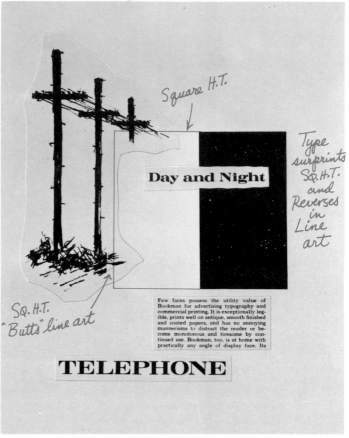

Square H.T.

Type surprints Sq. H.T. and Reverses in Line art

Day and Night

SQ. H.T. "Butts" line art

Few faces possess the utility value of Bookman for advertising typography and commercial printing. It is exceptionally legible, prints well on antique, smooth finished and coated papers, and has no annoying mannerisms to distract the reader or become monotonous and tiresome by continued use. Bookman, too, is at home with practically any angle of display face. Its

TELEPHONE

148 The one-board mechanical. All line art is mounted or drawn in position on the board. The drawing, which can be done directly on the board, overlaps the area of the square halftone (indicated for the platemaker by a blue outline). The type that surprints and reverses is mounted across the black panel. All elements are carefully specified.

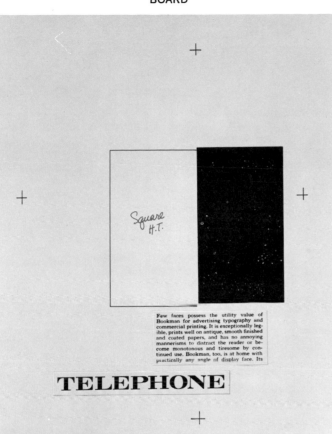

149 ...With overlay. The board contains the basic line elements and a normal red guide-line for the square halftone. A stat of the line drawing and the surprint/**reverse** type are mounted on the overlay.
Right: Original art for the square halftone is scaled and cropped in proportion.

CHAPTER 8

THE MECHANICAL: MULTI-COLOR PRINTING

Multi-color printing is the printing of more than one ink color on any single printing job. This requires, in addition to the different inks, a separate printing plate for each ink color. The stock will pass through the printing press once for each color, or, when two- or four-color presses are used, through a separate head—each with its own plate and ink rollers—for every ink color. To achieve an accurately printed multi-color job, the color plates must be printed in exact register in the precise relationship indicated by the sketch and defined by the mechanical.

Color printing may be divided into two major categories: *flat color* and *process color*.

Flat color is printing using available standard ink colors or ink mixed to match a color swatch. The color areas may be solid, or screened for tints, patterns or halftones; and they are reproduced from black-and-white original artwork.

Process color is the color reproduction of original art that has been executed in continuous-tone color. It is called four-color process, full-color process, or simply, process printing. Paintings and color photographs are examples of original art reproduced this way.

PRINTING INK

One of the basic ink characteristics, which is both a limitation and an advantage, is that most colored inks are quite transparent. This means that when one is printed over the other, the viewer will see two or more overlapping inks as a single color. Red over blue appears purple, blue over yellow appears green, etc. (Figure 150). Black will generally cover other ink colors, but it, too, is not totally opaque and a second color will show through black as a shine or an increased intensity of black. Some inks, mainly yellows, are semi-opaque and when printed over other colors have a tendency to become muddy: to overcome this problem of opacity, the more opaque inks are generally printed first. By overlapping the transparent ink colors, additional

150 The overlap of blue and red printing inks appears purple.

colors can be created without additional plates and press runs, which are the major elements in determining production costs.

FLAT COLOR

The limitation of transparent inks becomes obvious when one flat-color area is intended to touch another. In spite of the precision and accuracy of modern printing equipment, a certain degree of press movement must be tolerated in commercial production. When two color-areas touch, some press sheets will show a gap between the two colors, others will have a slight overlap of the colors. Both conditions are caused by the movement of the high-speed press. If the two contiguous colors are other than black, the overlap will be very obvious as a third color—the visual mixture of the two inks. We can only rely on the precision of the press and the ability of the pressmen to keep this overlap to a minimum. However, if one of the colors is black, an overlap is desirable and is provided for on the mechanical. Because black will cover the second color, the two color-areas will appear to meet exactly, and the possibility of a gap between the colors is eliminated (Figure 151).

RED

151 To produce this printed result the artwork for the red printing plate was made slightly wider than the portion visible here. This eliminated the possibility of a gap between the panels of color.

20%

SOLID

40%

60%

152 A black halftone printed over a solid color and three different tints.

Flat multi-color printing also permits screened areas of different colors to be printed over each other. The areas can be flat tints or a combination of halftone and tints. For example, a black halftone may be printed over a 20%, 40% or 60% tint of red (Figure 152)—a 40% tint of blue over a 60% tint of red, etc. (Figure 153). To make plates for overprinting screens, the platemaker must rotate the screen (change the angle) for one of the plates in order to

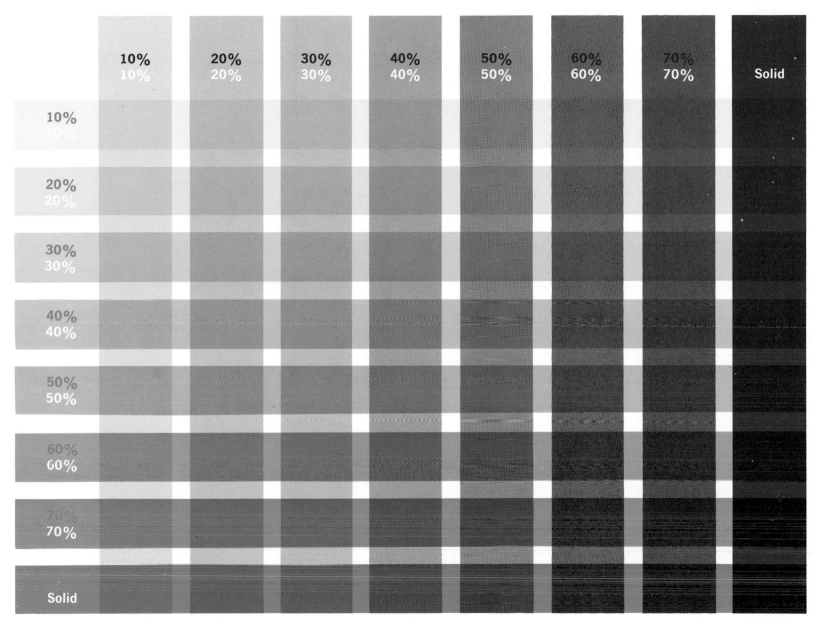

153 This chart shows the effect of overprinting the complete range of tints of blue and red. (MASTERCRAFT LITHOGRAPHERS, INC.)

avoid a moiré pattern. A moiré pattern is caused by the halftone dots overlapping irregularly, but when the screen angle for one plate is changed, the dots lie alongside each other without overlapping (Figure 154).

A duotone (called duograph by some photoengravers) is a two-color effect created from one black-and-white, continuous-tone original. Two separate halftone negatives, one for each color, are shot at different screen angles, with different tonal ranges, to achieve the desired shadow and highlight detail. Overprinting the two halftones results in a rich, deep, two-color halftone (Figure 155).

154 a. The moire pattern is caused by the incorrect angling of one of the halftone screens.

b. Correct screen angle permits the dots to lie next to each other and appear as an even, deep color.

155 A duotone is the result of overprinting half-tones of the same art in two colors. The halftone for each color is shot at a different screen angle and with different tonal ranges to achieve the maximum shadow and high-light detail, thus enriching the effect of the original photograph.

The Mechanical

PRE-SEPARATED ART. The ideal mechanical for flat multi-color printing requires the preparation of separate and complete artwork for each color. The most practical procedure is to prepare the art for the most complicated color, usually black, on an illustration board and to use a separate, transparent overlay for each of the other colors. To ensure accurate register of the colors, register marks must be placed on the board and on each overlay. A color swatch should be affixed to each surface for clear identification of the printing color.

This procedure, called pre-separated art, results in a mechanical in which each color is prepared separately and completely, ready for the camera. The platemaker simply makes a separate printing plate from the copy on the illustration board and from each overlay. The camera and stripping procedures are identical to those used for one-color jobs and the art is prepared in black and white with the same tools, media and elements. Color is achieved with the ink on the press and not in the preparation of the artwork (Figure 156).

The responsibility for fit, position, overlap, and register rests with the artist, so the art must be executed carefully and accurately. Pre-separated art results in the most economical multi-color printing plates since the platemaker's work and responsibility are at a minimum.

156 A three-color printing job, pre-separated for platemaking. The printed result is shown at (a). The copy on the illustration board (b) and on the overlays (c, d) are complete for each color. Three separate printing plates will be made.

b.

ALIVIO
RAPIDO
DE LA
GARGANTA IRRITADA

PASTILLAS
Cepacol

ATACAN LAS BACTERIAS—CALMAN LA IRRITACION
DE SABOR AGRADABLE

b.

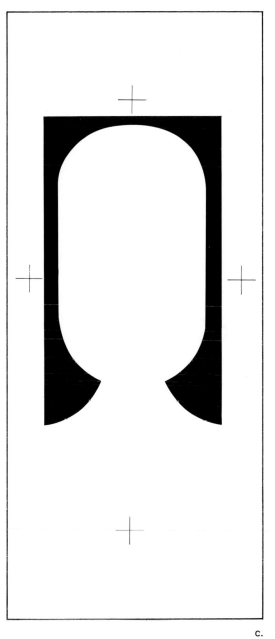

c.

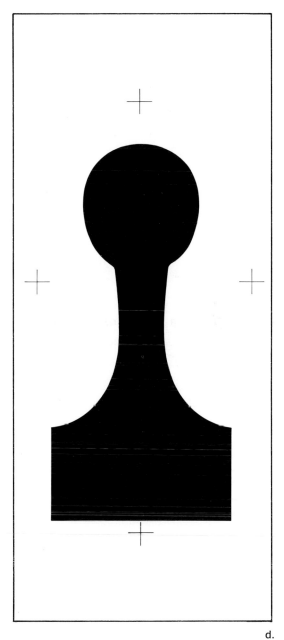

d.

KEY-LINE MECHANICAL. Multi-color artwork can also be prepared without any color overlays. This one-board, or key-line mechanical requires the platemaker to do the color separations. This involves much more extensive camerawork and stripping than with pre-separated art and consequently increases the cost of the plates.

There are at least two valid reasons for doing key-line mechanicals:

1. When the artist is pressed for time, key-line mechanicals can usually be done much more quickly than color separations without any sacrifice in reproduction quality.

2. If fit or register is extremely critical or delicate, it is best to use the key-line mechanical. Color separation becomes a photomechanical process, eliminating most elements of human inaccuracy.

To make a key line, a normal black and white mechanical is prepared on illustration board for the most involved color, usually black. Each of the other colors is then accurately outlined with red ink guide-lines (key lines) directly on the board.

The color separation is indicated to the platemaker on a tissue flap with colored markers or pencils (Figure 157). Working on the tissue flap – not on the board! – each area to be printed is indicated by filling in with an appropriate color. Exact ink-color swatches are still necessary for the printer. These should be mounted on the illustration board and keyed by name to the colors used on the tissue. A color sketch or dummy should be included with the artwork as further reference for the color separation.

The cameraman will photograph the entire key-line mechanical as many times as there are colors to be printed. This results in a separate negative for each color. On each negative, the stripper will opaque, block out, all the guide lines and art elements which do not apply to the particular color for which that negative is intended. A negative is prepared this way for each color. When two color-areas touch, a single, red guide-line will indicate the common boundary for each of the colors allowing the thickness of the line to function as an overlap.

Very often, a combination of color overlays and key lines will prove to be the most practical way to prepare a multi-color mechanical, both to economize in the platemaking and to ensure utmost accuracy (Figure 158). Each problem will determine its own particular solution. A careful analysis of the design or layout will usually reveal the best procedure for tackling the mechanical.

Color Proofs

Upon request, the platemaker or printer will supply color proofs for approval. The most accurate proofs are *press-proofs* which require printing plates and are therefore costly. *Color-keys* are proofs of each color on separate sheets of clear acetate. When placed on each other in register, they approximate the final printed result. Other forms of plastic color proofs, such as cromalin and transfer keys, are available as well.

157 a. This is a key-line mechanical for the same reproduction shown in Figure 156a. The black copy has been handled in the conventional way, but the red and blue copy have been indicated with red keylines.

b. The tissue overlay shows the color placement.

ALIVIO
RAPIDO
DE LA
GARGANTA IRRITADA

PASTILLAS
Cepacol

ATACAN LAS BACTERIAS—CALMAN LA IRRITACION
DE SABOR AGRADABLE

a.

b.

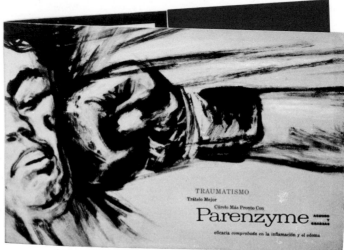

158 a. Rough dummy and final
printed copy of a folder.

164

b. The original continuous-
   tone art for the job.

c. Reproduction of one side.

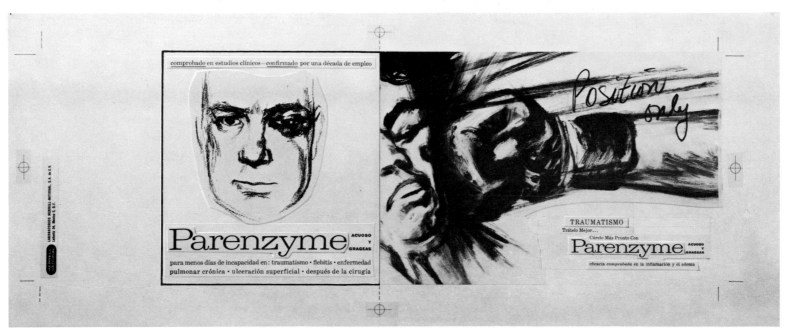

d. The mechanical utilizing key lines and overlay.

BOARD

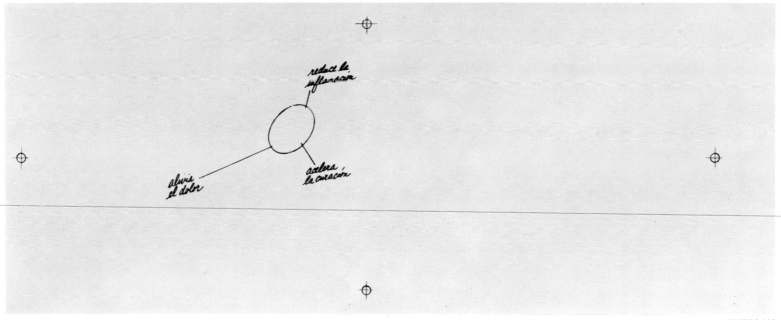

OVERLAY

COMPROBADO en traumatismo⁶⁶

Para la reducción rápida, espectacular, de la inflamación, el edema y el dolor—

Parenzyme
ACUOSO Y GRAGEAS

PROBLEMA "Ojos amoratados," contusiones y hematomas contraídos en deportes de contacto o que aparecieron después de la rinoplastia, tiroidectomía o disección del cuello.

PACIENTES 140.

PROCEDIMIENTO Parenzyme Grageas, 2 cada seis horas.

PRUEBA "...los resultados fueron buenos en 120 casos y dudosos en 20. Los resultados buenos se obtuvieron en los casos en que el edema y el dolor desaparecieron en 24 horas y el proceso se resolvió en 72 horas."

• "...el cambio de color en la equimosis de la piel, fue diferente — con la rápida aparición en 24 horas de un color rosa-rojo, en lugar del azul-negro pavonado que se observa en la equimosis no tratada."

• "El edema que circunda a las lesiones del tejido blando desaparece más pronto que en los casos no tratados."

• "El intenso edema subcutáneo y la hemorragia después de la rinoplastia, la tiroidectomía y las disecciones del cuello exhibieron una notable resolución en 24 horas."

• "Tres pacientes que tuvieron hemorragia intraocular debida a traumatismo experimentaron resolución de la hemorragia en 3 a 4 días."

TRAUMATISMO

DESORDENES VASCULARES PERIFERICOS

ENFERMEDAD PULMONAR CRONICA

ULCERACION SUPERFICIAL

CIRUGIA

e. Reproduction of reverse side.

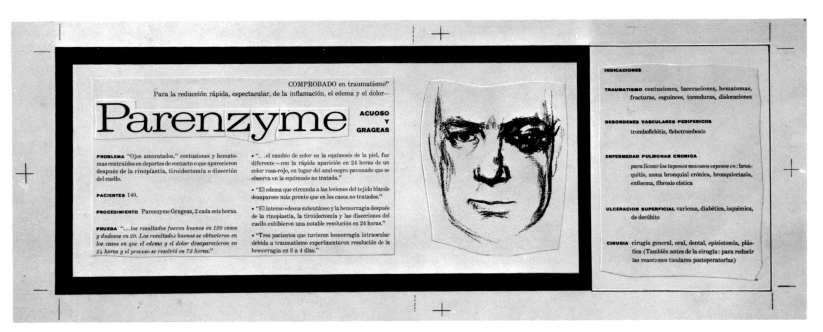

f. Mechanical for this reproduction with overlay.

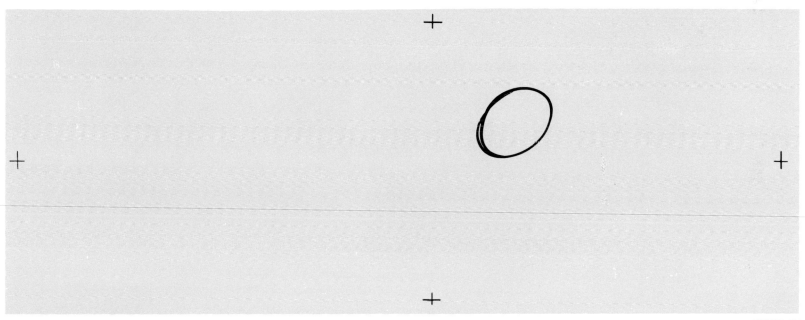

Color Guides

There are several aids, guides and tools available to help the artist see colors and color effects before the actual printing.

Each ink manufacturer publishes and distributes sample books with individual pages printed in standard colors. These inks are printed on both coated and uncoated stock. The pages generally have a series of perforated swatches which can be torn off and affixed to the mechanical as a color guide for the printer. As a further aid, each page usually shows a reverse, some copy printed in black over the color, and one or two tinted values of the color (Figure 159).

Other available color guides display the results of printing tints of one color over tints of other colors. Usually, the colors are limited to combinations of the four *process* ink colors used for full-color reproduction (see Chapter 9).

159 Ink manufacturers' swatch books.

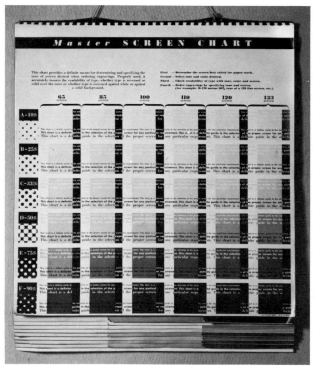

160 Engravers tint chart.

Matching Color System

The PANTONE® MATCHING SYSTEM is a method for the communication, selection, specification, matching and control of color and is comprised of a number of color reference books that coordinate the colors of markers, paper, film and specific ink formulations. Exact specification of ink colors to the printer are based on coded numbers which have become standardized throughout the printing industry. The colors are reproduced in swatch books and color guides (Figure 161) on both *coated* (glossy) and *uncoated* (dull) papers since there is a significant difference in the printed color. A variety of matching papers, transparent films and markers are available to produce comprehensive sketches and artwork for reproduction.

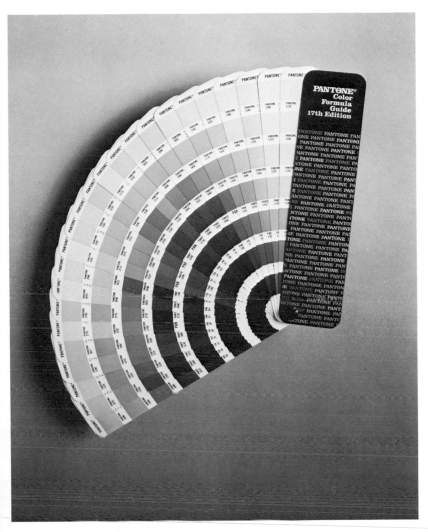

161 A Pantone color sample book

Bourges

Bourges is a color medium for the execution of color separated art. It consists of a series of transparent sheets which are coated with removable printing-ink colors. By removing, building up or simply cutting out sections of the color sheets, the artist is able to create color copy, in separate color overlays, which simulates the printed result (Figure 162). Since the art is color separated, each overlay is photographed individually as line or halftone copy. The overlays themselves can be used as color guides for the printer. Bourges sheets in values of gray and white can be used with photographs and drawings to change tonal values (Figure 163).

a.

162 a. Black key-drawing.

b. Bourges overlay. Portions of ink coating have been removed with a stylus.

c. Reproduction done from line artwork and Bourges overlay sheet.

163 a. An original photograph.

b. Effect produced by placing a 50 percent white Bourges sheet over the photograph and removing portions of the overlay to emphasize the subject.

c. The coating is removed from portions of a 50 percent gray Bourges overlay to highlight the subject.

a.

b.

from soup
to nuts

c.

b.

c.

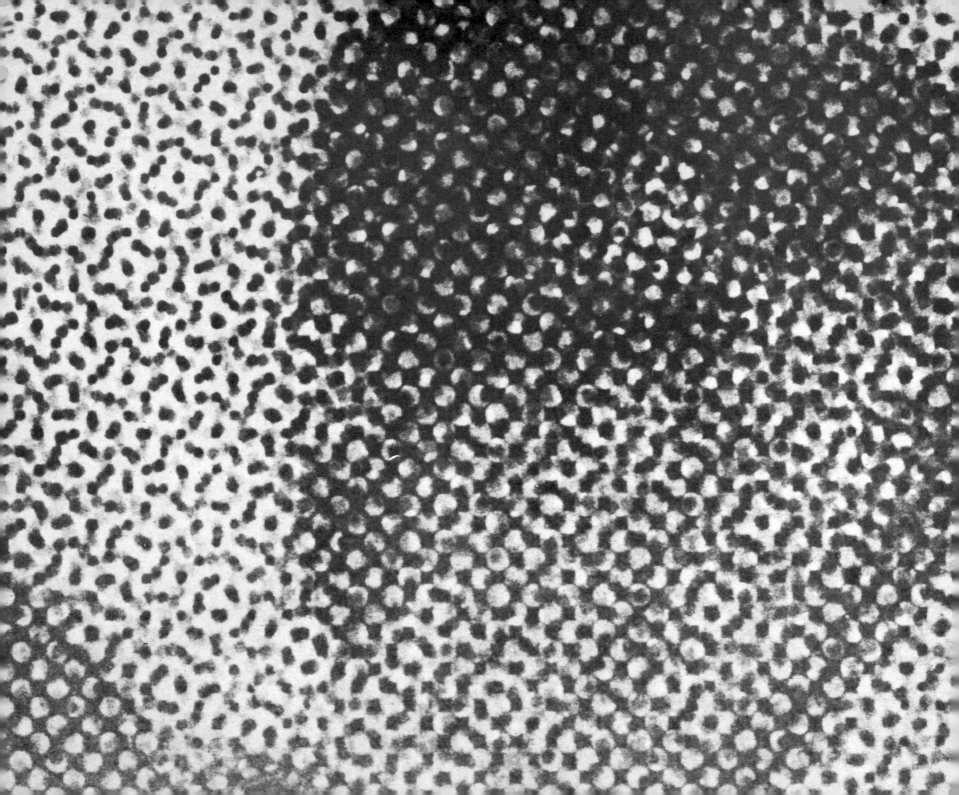

CHAPTER 9

PROCESS COLOR

Continuous-tone artwork in full color, such as paintings, color photoprints and transparencies are reproduced by process color printing. The process printing plates are achieved by the photomechanical separation of the primary colors—red, yellow and blue—which are elemental to all full-color art. Each process printing plate is a complete halftone plate of one of the primary colors, a duplication of the exact proportion and distribution of the color as it exists in the original subject. Since any desired color can be obtained by mixing the proper proportions of the primary colors, when these plates are printed over each other in precise register, they render a visually faithful, color-blended reproduction of the original.

Full-color reproduction may be achieved with just the three primary process plates: red, yellow and blue. However, a fourth halftone plate, black, is generally added to reinforce the detail, enhance the modeling, and to facilitate the reproduction of gray or neutral colors. This is four-color process printing (Figure 164).

SCIENCE OF COLOR

Though a full scientific understanding of light and color is not necessary to comprehend the principles of process printing, some fundamental information is helpful.

White light consists of waves of varying lengths and contains all the visible colors in the spectrum. Each individual color is associated with a different wave length. An object assumes a given color because it reflects that particular light wave and absorbs the rest. A sheet of red paper, for example, reflects red light waves but absorbs the others, while blue paper reflects only the blue waves. There are only seven principal colors visible in the light spectrum: red, orange, yellow, green, blue, indigo and violet. We see an infinite number of colors, however, because objects reflect different proportions and combinations of light waves, or, in other words, mixtures of colors. White paper reflects all the light waves, absorbing none, and the viewer sees the total reflection of the original white light.

The colors can be divided into the three principal additive primary colors of white light: red, blue and green. White light is composed of these colors and this can be demonstrated by projecting red, blue and green lights over each other on a white surface. Where two of these colors overlap, secondary colors (subtractive primaries) appear. These three colors—magenta, cyan, and yellow—are the ink colors used in the reproduction of color artwork (process printing) and are referred to as the process colors.

COLOR SEPARATION NEGATIVES

To make color separation negatives for a set of four-color process plates, the full-color art is photographed four times, once for each of the four component process colors of the final full-color reproduction: red, yellow, blue and black. Each photograph is made through a different color filter (the additive primaries) which "separates" the particular color to be recorded. A blue filter is used to produce a negative of the yellow portions of the artwork. The blue filter permits red and blue light reflected from the original to pass through and expose the film. All the yellow light is absorbed by the filter and does not reach the film. This results in a negative in which the yellow portions are transparent. When this negative is used to make a positive image, such as a printing plate, only the transparent portions of the negative will be recorded, in this case, only the yellow image. A green filter results in a negative for the red image, and a red filter records the blue. The black separation is made through a modified (yellow/orange) filter, which limits over-all color absorption, and produces a full-tone negative of the entire original.

This first step has produced four, color-separated negatives in continuous tone; the halftone screen has not yet been used. These negatives, already color corrected to some degree in the camera, are rephotographed or exposed onto photographic film to produce continuous-tone positives which are retouched to correct any color inaccuracies that may still exist. The retouched positives are then photographed through a halftone screen to create the four-color process, halftone negatives. A printing plate for each color is then made from each negative in the usual way (Figure 166).

Process halftone negatives can be produced in one photographic operation if a halftone screen is placed in the camera during the first step in the photographic color separation. This direct method, however, does not permit as much color correction control as the indirect method described earlier.

When the halftone negatives are made, the screen is rotated to a different angle for each color (Figure 167). This change in screen angle prevents the printed dots from interfering with each other and creating disturbing moiré patterns. The dots, in process printing, should lie next to each other so that they form perfect "rosettes" of the four colors (Figure 165).

164 Four-color process reproduction of a full-color photograph. (AMERICAN PHOTOENGRAVERS ASSOCIATION)

165 Enlarged section showing the halftone dot structure of four-color process printing.

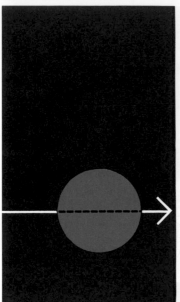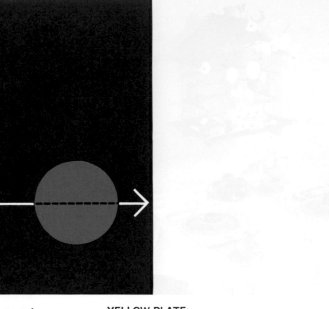

166 Color filters and reproductions from the color-separated process plates.

YELLOW PLATE:
THE ORIGINAL COPY IS PHOTOGRAPHED
THROUGH A BLUE FILTER.

RED PLATE:
THE ORIGINAL COPY IS PHOTOGRAPHED
THROUGH A GREEN FILTER.

BLUE PLATE:
THE ORIGINAL COPY IS PHOTOGRAPHED
THROUGH A RED FILTER.

BLACK PLATE:
THE ORIGINAL COPY IS PHOTOGRAPHED
THROUGH A MODIFIED FILTER
WHICH LIMITS COLOR ABSORPTION
AND PRODUCES A FULL-TONE NEGATIVE.

PROCESS INKS

The ink colors used in process printing are called process colors. They are a particular red (magenta), yellow (lemon yellow), and blue (cyan). The inks vary somewhat for the different printing processes and from different manufacturers, but they are all basically the same set of process colors.

MECHANICALS

In the preparation of a mechanical for process work, the size and position of the full-color reproduction is indicated in precisely the same manner as for any normal halftone, either with guide lines, solid form or photostat. A normal one-color or multicolor mechanical is prepared for all the other elements to be reproduced with the full-color art.

A variety of surprints or dropouts is possible in process work and, since there are four plates involved, surprints or dropouts must be very clearly specified, e.g., surprint of black; dropout of yellow and red only; dropout of all four colors; etc.

In addition to the actual process reproductions, the four, process ink colors are available for use as flat color in other areas of the particular piece being printed. The colors may be used singly or in combination to create any other desired flat color or effect.

167 Halftone screen-angles used in process platemaking.

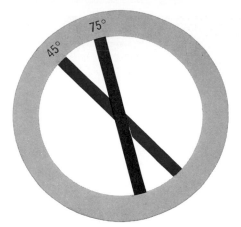

SCREEN ANGLES USED IN TWO-COLOR PROCESS

SCREEN ANGLES USED IN THREE-COLOR PROCESS

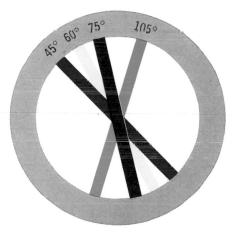

SCREEN ANGLES USED IN FOUR-COLOR PROCESS

Yellow

Yellow and red

168 Four-color process plates printed in sequence showing the progression of colors. Proofs of this progression, called progressive proofs or "progs," can be supplied with the plates so the reproduction can be checked for accuracy. Color-keys may also be used as progressive proofs in four color process printing (see page 162).
(AMERICAN PHOTOENGRAVERS ASSOCIATION)

Yellow, red and blue

Yellow, red, blue and black

CHAPTER 10

CONCLUSION

There are four fundamental stages in the development of a creative effort in printed communication:

1. The idea, concept, approach,
2. The design,
3. The mechanical, finished art,
4. Production.

An idea that never takes form is wasted, it might just as well not exist. To give graphic form to an idea requires the knowledge, the understanding and the ability to design. But the design will be of no value unless it can be translated into a mechanical. Therefore, to design intelligently demands the knowledge, the understanding and the craftsmanship necessary for the execution of the mechanical. And to prepare artwork for reproduction requires an intimate familiarity with the reproduction processes and techniques.

Each stage of the creative effort is dependent upon another. For instance, although the designer rarely prepares finished artwork and the production artist specializes in the execution of mechanicals, it is absolutely incumbent upon each to understand the other's job, and for both to understand reproduction.

Such understanding is acquired through study, and through experience for which there is no substitute. This does not necessarily mean only your own experience; take as much advantage of the experience of others as possible. Visit your typographer, platemaker and printer. They are cooperative, knowledgeable and experienced—your best sources of detailed information. One visit to a shop to watch a job in progress is an invaluable education.

And keep alert to new developments in the graphic arts. Technology and technique, materials and methods are advancing so rapidly, it is difficult to keep pace. As in any vital profession, the practitioner must be aware of current trends that affect his work. There are several excellent professional magazines that gather and disseminate this information regularly. They point to the direction of creative advance and explain the new levels of production progress.

Above all, remember that knowing why automatically tells you how. It is the authors' hope that this book has shown the Why and How of the preparation of art for reproduction and, as a permanent reference, will continue to fulfill its intended purpose.

INDEX

ABOUT THE AUTHORS

Arthur Eckstein and Bernard Stone, well-known graphic designers, have combined their outstanding talents and professional knowledge in writing *Preparing Art for Printing revised edition.* Their work covers a broad spectrum of design in virtually every medium of visual communications, including promotional literature, publications, packaging, corporate identity, TV, and films. Their designs appear in leading design journals and anthologies, and each has received recognition and numerous awards from professional organizations such as the Type Directors Club, the Art Directors Club, the Society of Typographic Arts, the American Institute of Graphic Arts, Society of Illustrators, the Creativity Shows, CLIO, and the New York International Film & TV Festival.

Mr. Eckstein teaches, lectures, and writes on the subject of graphic design. He is a member of the Package Designers Council and the American Institute of Graphic Arts. He has been listed in Who's Who in the East.

Mr. Stone is an instructor at Parsons School of Design and was an associate professor of graphic design at New York University. He is a member of the Art Directors Club of New York.

NOTES

NOTES

NOTES

NOTES